A CHANGING AMERICA:

at Work and Play

A CHANGING

NEW YORK · JOHN WILEY & SONS, INC.

London, Chapman & Hall, Limited

AMERICA:

at Work and Play

A. W. ZELOMEK

President, International Statistical Bureau, Inc.

Visiting Professor

The Graduate School of Business Administration

University of Virginia

81986

FOREWORD

This midtwentieth century period in American history is a very exciting one, and the excitement, as is usual, involves combined elements of fear, confusion, and bewilderment. And, of course, this period is quite different from any other. There is little resemblance between conditions today and those of postdepression 1939, of the period before the First World War, of the gay and prosperous 20's, or of the depression years which followed. Everyone will probably agree on one thing, that never before was there a time like the present. But raise the question, "What does it all mean?" and the usual result is a hot argument between opposing viewpoints.

Some of the excitement, as well as the fears and the conflicts of opinion, reflect the rapid pace of changes, particularly in the years since the war. Social and economic changes haven't taken place gradually, giving us all time to become accustomed to them. They have taken place with explosive rapidity and force, and they raise frightening questions. Was there ever such a mad rush to the suburbs? Will automated man be the slave or the master of the machine? Does the modern woman lose more in her family life than she gains in her career? Are we repeating the history of the 20's, and rushing madly toward a great depression? These and other questions have attracted the attention of specialists—economists, sociologists, psychologists, technicians of all kinds —as well as students, businessmen, and just plain people. Studies in depth have been made of automation, of suburbia, of modern woman, of all our midtwentieth century changes, and on any single one of these subjects the interested person can find extensive information; almost more information, in fact, than he can digest.

This intensity of interest is natural, and its results are generally good. These basic and explosive changes deserve the careful study they have received. Specialists have moved as rapidly to study the significance of these events, as the events themselves have moved in developing their significance. Yet when we ask what it all means, we still have the fierce and sometimes bitter conflicts of opinion.

Perhaps this too is natural and unavoidable. Certainly it is good that we have these reams of specialized information about very specialized and important developments. It is also possible, however, that our confusion and conflicting opinion betray a lack of perspective. It is not that we have too much information about individual events which causes confusion, but that we have too little about their related meaning. In "A Changing America," therefore, an attempt has been made to meet this deficiency.

I have approached this task with a great deal of humility. I have, of course, been compelled to prepare this material for publication. As a practical business economist, however, I have been compelled to inform myself about these developments, and to appraise their significance. The growth of suburbia has had an impact on buying patterns and consumer demand. It has involved an expansion in some cases, and a relocation in others, of basic industries, service and otherwise. The life pattern of the midtwentieth century woman has affected merchandising practices as well as family relations. The expansion of the service industries lends elements of stability to the economy, which are not yet fully recognized even by some professional economists. Automation will cause profound changes in productive processes and efficiencies, in the position of management and labor, and in the occupational pursuits of our growing population. A further increase in leisure time creates problems for the businessman as well as the sociologist. All of these changes are of direct interest to the business-man, and I, who have acted as a consultant to thousands of clients over a period of thirty-three years, have been compelled to interest myself in these developments as well as in the traditional economic elements of supply, demand, production, distribution, prices, money, foreign exchange, and political developments.

As I have been compelled in my business, and in the interest of my clients, to study these individual developments, their relationships, and their significance, it may seem natural that a book of this sort should have been the outcome. Actually, great credit is due others with whom I have been associated. They have contributed greatly by their interest.

I owe a particular debt of gratitude to the Graduate School of Business Administration of the University of Virginia. The Administration of the school believed that the graduate students, before going out into the business world, should be exposed to a series of lectures on the atmosphere of the American economy, which would deal with the same important events that are dealt with in this book, and I was invited to give these lectures. After I had prepared the lectures, it was not too difficult to expand them for publication. More important, I was persuaded to do so largely by the very real interest shown by graduate students and faculty alike. This interest encouraged the belief that there might be a broader audience for these topics, and that the additional labor of expansion and publication was justified.

The material presented here has been shaped and formed over a period of time, and the constant exchange of ideas I have had with my associate Dr. Robert C. Shook has been most helpful. Many of my clients, business associates, and professional friends in the fields of economics, sociology, and government have contributed their ideas and their interest. To all of them I am grateful.

For the extensive research which the book required— the amassing of information, its assimilation and analysis, and finally its organization—I am particularly indebted to Esther Highland, who bore most of this burden with great patience and good humor.

If a dedication of this work were to be made, it would be to an ideal rather than a person. There never has been a time like this before, and there never will be again. Perhaps, if there is a broader understanding of where we are now and how we got here, then what comes next may somehow be better for us all than it otherwise would have been.

A. W. ZELOMEK

November, 1958

CONTENTS

1 MODERN MAN

A Pause for Reflection

America in midcentury is truly a land of plenty. We measure our car ownership and our home ownership in millions, our population in hundred millions, our income and expenditures in billions. We travel fast and far, at home and abroad. We think of ourselves in superlative terms as the richest, the most highly industrialized, with the highest standard of living, the most powerful. Or, at least, we did. The postwar period, which brought such real prosperity for so many of our citizens, also saw some stones thrown in the pool of our complacency. The ripples are spreading, perhaps slowly, because the complacency is pretty thick and will not move easily.

Challenged by a growing power with a potential which we tried hard not to recognize, we are slowly becoming aware that we cannot live or lead by mass production and military might alone. We have no monopoly on technological competence or natural and human resources. We have been outstripped in some phases of scientific research and are being matched in others. Our position of leadership, which came easily, will have to be held through heroic effort.

If we are again to develop a unique standard—as we have with our standard of living—it will have to be in the area of ideas and values, not material things. We have realized the goal of more possessions and easier living which has motivated us as a nation, only to find that the old pressures and demands have been replaced by new and heavier ones. Despite widespread prosperity and unprecedented economic cushioning, our security is overlaid with insecurity; the "peace of mind" books reach the best-seller list, and drugs which promise "tranquility" become widely enough used to be familiar to a mass television audience.

Perhaps we have been so intent on reaching the goal of a better standard of living and have approached it so rapidly that, like the White Queen in *Through the Looking Glass*, we have run past it without stopping. Living as we do, in the second half of the twentieth century, it is difficult to realize that our present organization of society, our concept of the interrelationship between individuals and government, and our massive industrial plant have been less than a century in developing.

Until nearly the end of the nineteenth century, it was the general belief that the old industrial system, with all its shocking economic and social consequences, and the detachment of the government from the welfare of the people were destined to last indefinitely, with only minor modifications. But political, economic, social, and technological revolutions turned the well-ordered pattern of living upside down. The relative security of former days gave way to rapid, often undirected change.

Two major world wars, a wide and prolonged depression, the development of the automobile, the airplane and electronics, the release of women from the kitchen, the broadening of the educational base, all crowded into a short half century, have laid the foundation for a new order.

We have long been criticized as a purely materialistic society, frequently by foreign writers and recently by our own leaders in many fields. Much of the writing makes us sound as if we have given nothing to the world but the assembly line, forgetting all the basic rights of man which we proclaimed, fought for, and established. Not that the assembly line is a contribution to be disparaged [belittled]. The assembly line became the basis for a greater material good for a greater number of people. If a full supply of material goods does not necessarily assure the flowering of culture and brotherhood, it is certainly better to start toward Utopia in this way than with an empty stomach. Poverty and disease do not breed a race of philosophers.

The drives which founded and expanded the United States can be roughly summarized into the need for personal freedom and development, and the hope of material advancement. If the first need seems sometimes to be hidden under a mountain of goods and services, it is nevertheless still there, and can reassert itself, as it did in recent years. The United States, since its beginning, offered a haven from famine and from oppression. There is nothing wrong with the desire to do better than just escape famine, or to hope that our children will have a larger share of the country's produce than we had ourselves. The advancing standard of material progress, however, should be questioned when it tends to obscure other needs, when the benefits are inequitably divided.

or when the pressures engendered in the advance begin to counterbalance the benefits. How far have we come in the advance?

Consumption of goods, almost from the earliest days of the Union, was high, judged by contemporary European standards, yet it has increased rapidly ever since. Not much in the way of statistical evidence is available before the Civil War. Various studies show, however, that in 1860 real income was high in the United States as compared with Europe. The American standard of living, even at that time, included a greater amount of goods in every category of consumption, compared with other countries. The industrial revolution may not have originated in the United States, but certainly the United States has received the greatest benefits from this revolution and contributed most to its progress.

This leadership in living standards has been maintained throughout our history. Today real per capita purchasing power (that is, income after taxes have been deducted and after allowance has been made for the rise in the cost of living) stands 57 per cent higher than in 1929, a year generally regarded as a period of riotous prosperity. Nor does the use of an average figure hide extremes of wealth and poverty. More than ever before we have become a nation of middle-income families. A high level of economic activity, combined with a restricted labor force, minimum wage regulations, unionization, and unemployment and pension payments, has raised the level of the lower income groups. At the same time the tax structure, particularly the graduated income tax and inheritance taxes, has clipped the wings of the millionaires. As recently as 1941, 85 per cent of all spending units (persons living together who pool their incomes to meet major expenses) had annual incomes of

less than $3,000. By 1956 the proportion had been re-
duced to 33 per cent. Half the spending units were in
the $3,000 to $7,500 range, and they earned approximately half the nation's income. In 1941 the typical
middle-income family had an annual income of $1,458,
spent $1,017 on basic living costs, paid $2 in federal
income taxes, and had $439 left for discretionary spend-
ing. By 1958 the typical average income had risen to
$5,235. Basic costs for the same standard of living had
increased to $2,005, the federal government was taking
$415 in taxes, but the family still had $2,815 left for
discretionary spending.

What has pushed the economy of the United States
so much farther and faster than the economy of the rest
of the world? The traditional viewpoint recognizes the
fact that this country is rich in natural resources. Its
growth and its present high level of consumption are
therefore explained by the fact that people were willing
to work hard and take chances. Because the natural
resources were abundant, this hard work and risk-taking
led to increases in income, and therefore in consumption.

If this argument is logical and sufficient, how then can
we explain the comparative lack of progress in other
countries, notably in South America, but elsewhere as
well, who have had rich resources but have not developed a high level of consumption for the native popula-
tions? Let us try putting the traditional cart before its
horse and see whether the desire to consume can pre-
cede and bring about an increase in income.

The argument now runs thus: *Why U.S. Economy is as such:*

1. The American consumer has been anxious, from
the very beginning of the country, to increase his con-

sumption. This was, in fact, an important motive for
immigration.

2. The American consumer has found it possible,
by hard work and a willingness to take risks, to increase his consumption.

3. This combination of the desire to consume more
and the steadfast belief in the ability of the individual
to improve his position and increase his consumption
has therefore been the motivating force which distin-
guishes this country from all others and which has led
to the expansion of industry and the increase in national income.

We can at least find some evidence in history, if not
proof, of the importance of this personal element, this
desire to better one's position. Certainly the early set-
tlers and later immigrants must have believed strongly
in the ability of the individual to alter his position or
they would have stayed at home. Moreover, arriving in
this country, they found a society in which it was possible for a man, or his children, or his grandchildren, to
move up in the social and economic scale. The poten-
tialities of the developing country were widely advertised, not only by the big rags-to-riches successes but
also by small successes of obscure people known to many
of their friends.

Unlike the feudal economies of the old world, the
United States still had unowned land to be taken, distinction and wealth to be won in many fields, and no
stultifying belief that what was good enough for the
father must be good enough for the son. The waves of
immigration supplied the force for heavy, unskilled
labor. The native or second and third generation population moved up the scale to take over the semiskilled

jobs. The country's growth lines rose sharply, despite periodic pauses for depressions. Population, production, income, education, all expanded; only the hours of work and the amount of physical labor required declined.

Population

In the first half of this century alone, the population of the United States doubled. Starting out in 1900 with 76 million people, fed by immigration and aided by a declining death rate, the population reached 152 million by 1950 and 170 million by 1957. Within the framework of this growth, there have been two long-term trends which affect our social organization.

First, there has been a decline in the ratio of the number of men to the number of women. In 1900 there were approximately 104 males for every 100 females. The ratio rose slightly during the first decade of the century and then started a long-term decline which hasn't yet been interrupted. In 1956 there were only about 98 males for every 100 females, and that number includes the armed forces overseas, a problem American girls didn't have until after the Second World War.

The present surplus of women has resulted from two factors. Women live longer than men, and immigration which used to bring new supplies of men from overseas has been virtually cut off. Around the beginning of the century immigration averaged about 800,000 a year and was predominantly male. Now immigration runs around 150,000 and is about 60 per cent female.

Fortunately for the American girl, the preponderance of women is not true for all age groups. Up to the age of 24 there are still slightly more men than women, but, after that, the ratio goes down, until between the ages of 45 and 64 there are only 96 men to every 100 women, and after that only 86. The probability that sooner or later there will be no man around to support her is one of the forces bringing women back to work today.

The second long-term trend is the aging of the population resulting from the progress of medicine and the steadily rising life expectancy. A baby born in the United States today has a life expectancy of 70 years, some 22 years more than at the beginning of the century. The median age of the population has risen from 19 years in 1850 to 23 years in 1900, to 30 years today. Almost 9 per cent of our population today is 65 years old or more. By 1975 the Bureau of the Census predicts this proportion may increase to 10 per cent, depending on what course the birth rate takes in the next couple of decades.

Thus we shall have a larger and larger group of people (most of whom will be consumers without being producers), who will require specialized services for health, recreation, and housing, and who will stimulate research —social and medical—in geriatric problems. The belief is growing that the older portion of our population has the right to live, not just to exist, and public and private pension plans are helping them do it. Their needs will help to absorb the labor force which will be coming of age in increasing numbers during the next decade.

The Family

Despite the fact that, statistically speaking, we have more time to live, we seem to be in more of a hurry to marry and start having children than ever before. War and prosperity have both influenced this trend, war by stimulating the "now or perhaps never" feeling, prosperity by making marriage and children economically easier. Today the typical bridegroom is 23 years old, the bride 20. Back in 1890 the groom was 27, the bride 22. However, most of the drop has occurred since the beginning of the Second World War; until then the age levels had remained almost static.

Children are born earlier, the last one, typically, six years after the parents' marriage. The birth rate, which showed a long-term decline until 1940, zoomed during the war and, somewhat unexpectedly, continued up afterwards. Fortunately, the divorce rate, which also zoomed during the war, has declined slowly but steadily since then. The marriage and birth rates, which are currently slowing down, will again turn upward as the war and early postwar babies reach maturity and settle down.

The changes in family life which can be measured by statistics are only part—and the least spectacular part—of the full change in the daily life of the American family. At the beginning of the century the husband, wife, and children "knew their place," and this meant not simply knowing it but staying in it. The husband provided the family income, controlled its use, dominated his wife (or so he thought), and commanded his children. He worked long, hard hours to provide as well as he could for the family's needs and had time or thought for little else. His wife, if she worked at all before marriage, stopped when she married, bore and raised children, tried to establish a comfortable home, and aspired to win honors in cooking contests, not in careers. The children were seen and not heard.

Whether these were the *good* old days or not is a subject that can be argued indefinitely without reaching even a compromise conclusion. But the fact is that they were the old days and that, except for occasional survivals, the established "pecking order" and discrete functions of the members of the family are gone. Husbands have learned to change diapers, shop for the family's food, and be pretty efficient baby sitters. Wives frequently work until the first child is born (literally), often return to work when the children are in school, and are active politically and in the community as well as in the home and church. Children are not only heard as well as seen, but often command and are obeyed.

When father comes home from work it's at a much earlier hour, he has the week-end off, and he has both the time and energy left to wonder which demands to satisfy during his increased leisure. He is expected to be a pal to his son (although the son may prefer boys of his own age). He is expected to want to fix the plumbing because "all men like to putter and are mechanically inclined." He is expected to be active in school, church, and community affairs because isolationism is becoming as outmoded in personal life as in national affairs. He is expected to provide not only the necessities of life but also as many of the additions that have become necessities, or are still semi-luxuries, as he possibly can.

He can no longer feel satisfied if he sees his children through high school and then expects them to provide for themselves, and perhaps even for him. If they have any educational aptitude, he would like to see them through college. He has little worry about providing the necessities that his grandfather worked so hard for, but so much more is now expected of him that the pressure to provide is probably greater now than it was then. The fact that it can be done (as can be demonstrated by any number of neighbors with extra cars, multiple television sets, and winters in Florida) makes it imperative that he prove that he can do as well.

When mother settles down to marriage and children, she no longer feels that this is necessarily the only job she was meant for, or the only one she is likely to have during her lifetime. She was probably trained for something quite different and may have held a stimulating job before marriage. At least she spent her time in a world of adults, of action, of varied topics of conversation. She is likely to feel isolated and bored, but she may not know at what age she can leave her children and return to work without depriving them of essential care. She has much greater freedom than her grandmother had to choose her function in society, but she must face the emotional pressures and doubts which are part of either choice.

Yet, with all the rapid changes within the family, and the fact that many question the wisdom of the changes and label our reforming family homogenized like peanut butter, there is a new closeness and importance in family life and in the family's time together. (The word together is used here without any of the compulsive and cloying connotations of the current term "togetherness.") There is more time and more money for family vacations, and more space available in suburban homes for the family to play together. The importance of housing, which is expected to provide essential privacy as well as essential communal space, is evidence of today's emphasis on the relation of the members of the family to each other.

Labor and Productivity

The economic basis for all the rapid social and financial changes has been the technological advances that
have increased productivity of labor, in agriculture, mining, and manufacturing. Historically, the gain in output
per man hour has averaged about 2.5 per cent a year. In
recent years, however, the gain has been more rapid
than the long-term average.

The revolution in farm productivity has out-stripped
other sectors of the economy in the last 15 to 20 years.
Since 1940 agricultural productivity has about doubled
while output per man-hour in industry rose about 40
per cent in the same period. Today an American farm
worker supplies the agricultural needs of approximately
22 people, compared with less than 12 prewar. This rise
in productivity, due largely to new machinery and new
fertilizers, fungicides, and insecticides, has resulted in a
drastic population shift from the farm to the city during
this period. In 1940 there were 30 million people living
on farms, 101 million off farms. By 1957 the farm population had been reduced by nearly 10 million, the off-
farm population had been increased by 50 million.

The decline in agricultural employment helped meet
the needs of manufacturing and service industries during the war years and during the 1950's, when the number of adults entering the labor market was exceptionally low. It also added to the burden of the cities, which
could not provide adequate housing, and thus was an
additional factor in pushing the population from the
cities into the suburbs.

Technological changes in industry caused another
major shift in employment, an upgrading of labor away
from unskilled manual jobs to semiskilled, skilled, and

white-collar jobs. In 1910 the labor force was 31 per
cent farmers, 37 per cent blue-collar workers, and 22 per
cent white-collar workers. By 1956 the proportion of
farm workers was down to 10 per cent, and the proportion of white-collar workers—40 per cent—had caught
up with and just passed the proportion of blue-collar
workers.

The status of labor has been upgraded in other ways.
From the time when the sweat shop was accepted as
part of manufacturing and the worker was regarded as
a pair of hands, we have advanced to the acceptance of
wage and hour laws, control over conditions of work, the
right of labor to economic security in the form of unemployment benefits, pensions, and a guaranteed annual
wage. Hours of work, excluding overtime, have declined, earnings have gone up, and paid vacations and
holidays are the rule.

The rise of the labor unions was essential to the improvement of labor's position, but the growth of their
power was faster, in some cases, than control over their
leadership or their acceptance of responsibility. Today
they face the probability of government control and the
fact that, for economic reasons, they have probably
reached the peak of their growth. Future automation
will decrease the need for unskilled and semiskilled
workers, while increasing the need for engineers, pro-
gramers, highly skilled maintenance men, management
personnel. As an official of the Ford Motor Company is
said to have pointed out, machines do not pay union
dues, and, it should be added, engineers and junior executives are not as good material for union organization
as factory workers. The shift in employment from production to service industries will also weaken the potential for unionization.

But the unions no longer stand alone in their function of protector of the working force. Since the depression of the 1930's the government has become firmly established in its right to control minimum conditions of labor, to act as employment agency and as an insurance firm for unemployment relief and retirement benefits. The large corporations have also assumed a paternalistic role in regard to labor, partly to attract personnel during the war and postwar tight labor market, and also to stave off unionization. Company pension systems, severance pay, educational and cultural facilities—in general an acknowledgment of responsibility—have progressed to the point where retrogression is unlikely even when the labor market eases during the 1960's.

The Balance Sheet

The rising productivity of labor enabled industry to grant higher wages, shorter hours, and fringe benefits while still making a profit. As a nation, we have taken the benefits of the increase in productivity in increased time off from work and increased purchasing power. Per capita purchasing power (after allowing for taxes and the rising cost of living) has climbed with only minor interruptions since 1948 and today is 61 per cent above the prewar level.

How do we spend our money? Are we saving much of our new wealth, or have our needs increased with our incomes?

Except for the war years when merchandise was not available, and the immediate postwar years when people were catching up on their buying, the proportion of disposable income that has gone into savings has run between 6 and 8 per cent. At today's high rate of income, this amounts to approximately 20 billion dollars a year, almost five times the amount saved in 1929. Distribution among the population, of course, is uneven. Nearly one-quarter of all spending units have no liquid assets at all; almost one-third more have $500 or less. Older people hold a much larger proportion of savings than their proportion in the population because they have had more time to achieve financial stability and because their generation had to depend on itself for security instead of taking for granted the paternalism of government and corporation.

For the younger couples the proverbial rainy day has become a threat that can spoil a picnic. To them the deep depression of the 1930's is a chapter in a history book and seems quite unreal and impossible of repetition. We may have recessions, but the feeling is that "someone will do something about it." The government has provided shock absorbers through the Social Security system, and the people have probably provided for some emergencies through prepayment plans, like hospital insurance. Cash in the bank seems to be the least essential part of being able to buy. They are generally so secure in today's job and tomorrow's raises that they seldom hesitate to buy now and pay later, with little regard to what they are actually paying in added interest charges. The small amount of cash and government bonds on hand remains untouched for sudden and extreme emergencies; lesser needs are covered by personal loans.

Total installment credit (for automobiles, other consumer goods, repair and modernization loans, and personal loans) is now around 33 billion dollars, almost half for automobiles and another quarter for other consumer goods. The total has more than doubled since 1950, the biggest increases occurring for automobile and personal loans. The 15 billion dollar installment debt for automobiles is a reflection of the spread of the suburbs, where the car becomes a necessity. Automobile debt alone amounts to 5 per cent of disposable income.

More than half of all families, regardless of income, owe some installment debt, although about half of these owe $500 or less. There is a marked increase in installment buying when the family's income reaches and passes $3,000 a year. In families with incomes between $4,000 and $10,000, almost three-quarters owe some installment debt, one-third or more owing over $500. In spite of this increased credit spending, the nation's personal balance sheet is in good order. Total financial assets have increased more than debt, which more than doubled since 1950.

Some interesting comparisons can be drawn from an analysis of how we spend our money. Out of a total of 284 billion dollars spent in 1957, more than half went for the essentials like food, clothing, shelter, and household operation. Transportation took approximately 36 billion dollars, an amount comparable to our expenditures for housing. Recreation in all forms took 16 billion dollars. In the same year that we spent 15 billion dollars for smoking and drinking, we spent 7 billion dollars on research and development, both private and government, and most of government research is for national security. In the same year that we spent 42 billion dollars for national security (excluding research) we spent 18 billion dollars on education, private and public.

For a while it seemed as if research and education would finally be recognized as part of national security, but the enthusiasm for aid to education and basic research seems to have faded quietly, and the recent law to aid education is narrower than it should have been. It now looks as if it will take a Soviet man-on-the-moon to rekindle the fire.

Midcentury American Profile

* We are big.

Our population is 170 million and is expected to reach at least 207 million by 1975. We talk about mass communications, mass culture, mass media, and a middle-class mass market. Big business has developed mass production to its present peak, so that the question is no longer what do we need more of, but how shall we sell all we shall be able to produce. Advertising expenditures have jumped from a prewar level of 2 billion dollars to the current annual rate of 10 billion dollars. For every man, woman, and child in the United States, industry spends approximately $60 a year to raise the level of consumer needs, and to keep our production flowing swiftly through the channels of distribution.

Large corporations are part of the American economy, but are not as dominant as often thought. It is true that the largest 100 manufacturing concerns account for 30 per cent of production, and that in a variety of industries (aluminum, telephone and telegraph equipment, soap and glycerin, cigarettes, synthetic fibers, motor vehicles) the top four companies produce between 75 and 100 per cent of total shipments. On the other hand, even in manufacturing, there are important industries (paper and paperboard, construction and mining machinery, machine tools, leather, coats and suits, plastic products) where the top four companies account for less than 20 per cent of production.

For many reasons the concentration of industry in large companies seems less threatening today than when the antitrust laws were first passed. The stock of the large corporations is widely and publicly owned. The rise of the middle class and the more equitable distribution of income have been accomplished at the same time as the growth of the big companies. It is recognized that the economies of mass production accrue to the benefit of the consumer as well as the producer, and for some industries production would be economically impossible for a small company.

The progress of big business does not mean that the frontiers of business are closed to newcomers. There may be less opportunity to turn a shoe string into a million dollars, but there is still room for the man who prefers to be his own boss. Approximately 135,000 new businesses were incorporated in 1957, whereas the rate of failures was about 10 per cent of this amount. Many of the service industries which have become so important—the beauty shops, repair centers, small retailers, motels, advertising agencies, job printers—all offer business opportunities where success does not depend on size. The decentralization of the population into the suburbs and beyond will produce new opportunities for small business.

• We are mobile.

Our social and economic mobility have been a prime attraction since colonial days. Living in a country developed by people who undertook hazardous journeys for gold or land, and by immigrants who had the courage to start in a new country, we point with pride to the rail

splitter who became president and the penniless immi-
grant who became a millionaire. Since most of us trace
our ancestry to the melting pot rather than the May-
flower, roots and family trees are relatively unimportant.
The farmer goes to the city if the opportunity is more
promising. The young man leaves the small town where
he was born to go to college and probably won't return,
even if his family is well known locally and has lived
there for generations. The young executive moves himself and his family at the behest of his corporate employer, or, if the opportunity presents itself, he moves
from one job to another without too much worry about
its location. The growing family moves to a bigger
house. The family with improving income moves to a
more expensive suburb.

When most Americans lived in rented quarters, home
ownership represented stability, but despite the high
rate of home ownership today, we are still moving. In
the five years between 1950 and 1956, 156 million people
changed their place of residence, a total almost equal to
the entire population of the United States. Almost two-
thirds moved to a different house in the same county,
with the remaining one-third almost equally divided between those who moved to a different county in the same
state and those who moved to a different state.

In our daily lives we also move far and fast. We travel
longer distances, mostly by car, to reach our work. We
take planes to keep distant business appointments. A
vacation means going some place, not relaxing at home.
Active sports are more popular than spectator sports.
The man of action and obvious accomplishment is the
one to emulate; the scholar and the "egghead" are con-
signed to the ivory tower without much feeling of loss.

* We are subject to change without notice.

The terms we use in talking about the last twenty-five years—the income revolution, the technological revolution, the population explosion, the rush to the suburbs— recognize the accelerated pace with which change now occurs. Unfortunately, technology has outrun social development. We have developed atomic power but cannot control its use. We are reaching for the moon without being sure whether this is a challenge which the human mind must meet or a Soviet threat that the military machine must meet.

In fact, our society is full of contradictions. We have unprecedented wealth and too few schools. We have laws to encourage residential building, but the slums creep further. We have a rising level of education and want our children to go to college, but teachers get small social or financial compensation. We have more leisure but are often not satisfied with the way we use it. We talk about the value of the individual and of creative thought and exact conformity as the price of acceptance. We have the most economically cushioned society in history; secure in this respect we are threatened with the annihilation of atomic war.

Perhaps the very rapidity of change and progress during the first half of the century has left us floundering. A pause is in order, not so much for criticism as for reappraisal. Should we continue to emphasize greater production and consumption regardless of what is produced and consumed? Are there areas of our national life which must be considered essential although not self-supporting, like the performing arts? Shall we take the coming benefits of automation in the form of more leisure and more goods and services, or recognize that part of it must be skimmed off for the support of the older portion of our population and the poorer nations of the world? The following chapters, by considering some of the dynamic forces in our society, in retrospect and prospect, will help in this reappraisal.

2 | MODERN WOMAN

The Strength
of the Weaker Sex

*And the Lord God called unto Adam, and said unto
him, . . . Hast thou eaten of the tree whereof I commanded thee, that thou shouldest not eat?*
*And the man said, The woman whom thou gavest to
be with me, she gave me of the tree, and I did eat.*

That's how far back men started blaming their trou-
bles on their wives, and they haven't stopped since. As
part of her punishment for henpecking her husband in
this fashion Eve was condemned to have Adam rule over
her. But this dictum has become harder and harder to
carry out since the first girl was taught to read and found
she could do it as well as her brother.

The question of women's status in our social order is
one on which everyone has an opinion, frequently ill
considered and purely emotional. If it were possible to
view the situation from the sexless state of an ameba or
with the traditionless point of view of a Martian, it might
be easier to arrive at a balanced conclusion. Since this

is patently impossible, the battle of the sexes is fought in cartoons—barbed rather than funny—and in family television programs, where husband and wife are perpetually engaged in petty arguments or mother cleverly manages to outwit a good-natured boob of a father.

"The American woman is a major problem today," said a French bachelor in a particularly vitriolic article which appeared in the usually circumspect *New York Times*. I would rather say the American woman *has* a problem, the problem of how to fit together the many jobs which she must or wants to do, how to achieve self-fulfillment and retain the approval of society. The rigid standards of feminine behavior which were torn apart by the feminist movement have not yet been remodeled into a satisfactory pattern. The ideal of the fainting female is gone, but the growing girl is not quite sure who has taken her place.

Historical Development

In the days when the West was being opened and American society was chiefly agrarian, women were scarce and their price, in the form of social status, was high. The woman as well as the man performed productive functions without which the family could not exist. She was wife, mother, and homemaker, three functions completely intertwined, one following the other as surely as night follows day.

With the development of the industrial revolution, the productive function moved from the home to the factory. Husbands, except for those who remained farmers, moved out to the factory as well, while the wife remained in her "natural" place, at home with the children. In a society becoming more and more complex she was

expected to confine her thoughts and activities within
the walls of her home except if she chose to indulge in
ladylike charities.

This was the ideal, but it was not always followed.
Freedom and equality, the battle cry of the nation,
proved to be contagious. By the midnineteenth century
there was an active and successful movement underway
to get legal and educational equality for women. During
the First World War women were drawn out of the
home into the factories and even the armed forces as a
patriotic duty. By 1920 they had the franchise, and after
that progress toward full legal equality was rapid.

The early feminists and suffragettes were crusaders
not sociologists. Like many revolutionaries they over-
simplified the problem they were trying to solve. They
believed that equality would guarantee happiness and
that if they could compete on an equal basis in a man's
world they would automatically get social status with
legal rights. They tried hard to bypass basic biologic
differences and minimize childbearing as if this were
another form of slavery invented by men.

It didn't work. Much of the new code of conduct was
strictly in imitation of men's privileges and was indulged
in just to demonstrate equality. But equality should
never have been taken to mean imitation. This is an area
in which a doctrine of "separate but equal" could have
been properly applied. Biologic differences cannot be
legislated away (and who wants to!), and most women
not only want to have children but also want to raise
them. If, in addition to equal rights, women had been
given equal status, equal recognition for the job they
performed, the victory would have been more fruitful.

What has happened to the triple but inseparable role
of our pioneer woman?

A wife today has little prestige, being popularly satirized as scheming, improvident, grasping, domineering, giving her husband ulcers and heart attacks in exchange for a mink coat and diamonds.

A housewife today has turned over part of her function to prepared foods, mass-produced clothing, and electric appliances. The part that's left is the most unrewarding kind of maintenance work, like the housecleaning that nobody notices unless it's not done. The appliance advertisements which emphasize how easy everything is nowadays and the ladies who clean house on television in fancy dresses leave today's housewife on the defensive, a little uneasy herself about what she does with her time.

A mother today is drowned in canned sentiment and lilacs one day a year, and although she still has considerable status in this role, she has lost much of her security in performing it.

When great-grandma brought up her large family, her wisdom in child-rearing was seldom questioned. She rocked the cradle secure in the knowledge that she was ruling the world and doing it properly. If a child didn't turn out just right there was always a family skeleton in the closet (preferably her husband's family) for the child to "take after." She had done all that a good mother should, and there were usually enough proper children in the family to prove it.

Then came psychiatry with its emphasis on the importance of the infant's first experiences and the child's sense of security. The pendulum swung, and mother, who stood in its path, was cut down to a pretty small size. She was now told when to feed, how to feed, when to pick up the baby, when to put it down, when to love it, and when to diaper it. Now if anything went wrong it was her fault; she had been given a lump of clay and had modeled it badly.

It can be argued, with validity, that no job is more creative and should be more fulfilling than bearing and rearing children, but it's a little difficult for a woman to remember it during the daily routine of dishes and diapers in the conversational world of a two-year-old. It is particularly difficult to remember it in a society which rewards individual achievements and aggressive action, and frequently equates human value with the size of the pay-check.

Good evidence that "woman's work" carries with it little prestige is seen in the frequent ridicule directed at a man in the kitchen or nursery. Even if his own daily job consists of the most routine and undemanding work, he is considered to have lowered himself by taking over some of his wife's chores. On the other hand, a woman with a slide rule may be criticized for being unfeminine but certainly not for doing a job that's beneath her.

More evidence—if it is needed—is in life insurance data. Approximately 85 per cent of all life insurance policies are bought by men, only 8 per cent by women, and the average value is more than four times as great for men as for women. The implication is that economically, at least, a woman's work has little value and she can be easily replaced.

Motivation researchers have suddenly discovered that women need approval for their work. Why just women? Isn't it an elementary rule of good labor relations, for men as well as women, that good work should receive recognition? In business a man may get his recognition in many ways, in a raise, a gold watch, a promotion, a better job. A woman working at home has to wait for a kind word. It is not surprising then that more and more women look for prestige and recognition outside the home, usually, although not necessarily, in paid employment.

Education for What?

How is the girl educated for the several jobs she is expected to perform in our society?

Early in life she learns that her first big job is to get married—not so much to stay married, and to make a home, but simply to get a man! The revolution in sex standards has no doubt reduced the famous old ratio of "one fallen woman to a hundred fallen men" to a more nearly 50–50 basis but in one important respect the double standard remains unchanged. When a man doesn't marry he is presumed to have been too smart to get caught or to have chosen the bachelor state because it suits him. When a woman doesn't marry it is presumed that she didn't have what it takes (37–23–34) to get a husband.

For this job she gets some training and help. She is bombarded with advertisements and products designed to help her fulfill the glamour role. Her parents will supply the necessary powder, paint, perfume, and clothes if they can and will teach her how to make the spider web attractive to the fly.

Her second and third major jobs are running a home and bringing up children. To these all-important undertakings she comes armed with a junior high school course in home economics, a three-weeks' course in baby care practiced on a rubber doll, and a paperbound volume of Dr. Spock's book on baby care. Neither her mother nor her schools have thought it necessary to train her for this work. It is apparently something that anyone can do, and on-the-job training with no supervisor will be sufficient.

Her formal education may include specialized vocational training which she will use in the years between graduation and the arrival of her first child and then lay away, perhaps to be picked up again when the last child is in school. In school she is taught to develop whatever abilities she has, just as a boy is. In school she may have her first taste of individual achievement, just as a boy does. But for most girls the similarity ends there. The boy goes on to make whatever mark he can along the lines for which his training and ability suit him. The girl is expected to drop it all and be perfectly happy, submerging her own individuality in becoming Johnny's mother, for that is the identity she will have for many years, at least among the junior members of her society.

Thus a girl may be taught skills that she will use little or never, but she gets no training for the one job which society expects of her and which she probably wants to do.

Women Who Work

One great advantage that today's emancipated woman has over her sister of the nineteenth century is that she now can move freely outside her home, in a wide range of community activities and in paid employment. If she must support herself, she is no longer expected to stay in a relative's home in the status of an unpaid servant. However, if she works when she has young children and isn't forced to by economic need, the reaction of society is mixed and many of the questions and doubts come from within herself.

The rising tide of women entering or returning to the labor force is as much a social revolution as an economic one. Time was when a woman, particularly a married woman, worked outside her home only out of sheer necessity, usually in a factory and mostly among the lower economic classes. Higher up the income ladder, a man took pride in the fact that he could keep his wife at home. If he climbed high enough, he could not only keep her at home but also supply enough household help to keep her useless. She then became his status symbol and a form of "conspicuous waste" which was supposed to prove that he was successful in a manner which the culture deemed worthy of respect.

Fortunately this attitude is changing, although it has by no means disappeared. Women work for many reasons today, and even the economic need, which is still most important, has a much broader definition than absolute necessity.

Back in 1890 only 4 million women worked; this was 18 per cent of the total female population 14 years old and over. Only 4 per cent of the married women worked. By 1956 there were 21 million women in the labor force, or 35 per cent of all adult women; 24 per cent of all married women were working. As a result, the composition of the labor force had undergone a remarkable change. The proportion of women in the labor force had risen from 17 per cent in 1890 to 32 per cent in 1956. The number of married women living with their husbands and working was actually higher than the total of widowed, divorced, separated, and single women. Two out of five women, married, living with their husbands and having children of school age, are in the labor force.

For most working women the pattern of employment

is a three-stage operation; work between the end of education and the beginning of childbearing, home for a period of years, and then back to work. The largest proportion of women working outside the home is in the 18 to 24 year age group, 46 per cent. The proportion then drops sharply between 25 and 34 years to 35 per cent but goes right back up for the 35 to 54 year group to 44 per cent.

The most notable feature of an analysis of the female labor force is the increase in the proportion of women over 35 years who are employed. In 1940 just a little over a quarter of all women between 35 and 54 were working; by 1956 the proportion was nearly one-half. For the 55 to 64 year group the proportion rose during the same period from 18 per cent to 37 per cent. There has even been an increase in the group over 65 years, from 7 per cent to 11 per cent.

Chance for Advancement

For the many who fear that the mass entry of women into the business world will destroy the last stronghold of male supremacy there is great comfort in the occupational statistics. Although it is true that women have reached the status of bank president, department store president, cabinet officer, and senator, the majority are concentrated in occupations which men are happy to stay out of either because they are underpaid, unspecialized, or undervalued. In 1957, 30 per cent of all working women were in clerical work, 17 per cent were operatives (factory workers), and 24 per cent were service workers. Only 12 per cent were classified as professional workers, and 6 per cent were managers, officials, and proprietors.

The divergence between male and female occupational roles is found not only in kind of work but also in degree of advancement. Even in teaching, which includes the largest number of professional women and is generally considered a woman's profession, the high-ranking positions go mainly to men. Women make up 75 per cent of all elementary and secondary school teachers, but the proportion is much smaller on college faculties and in administrative posts. For example, a 1950 survey showed that fewer than 10 per cent of junior and senior high school principals were women.

There are many reasons for this difference, none of which relates to innate ability. The most important reason is that the majority of women do not intend to pursue an uninterrupted career and therefore do not undertake the more lengthy courses of study. A girl in school today may actually spend 25 years in employment outside her home, but she is likely to plan only on working until she has children. If she actually does this and stays out of the labor force for ten or fifteen years she has lost that much experience and seniority compared with a man who started out at the same spot.

If a woman wishes to pursue an uninterrupted career, she must either give up marriage or children, which most women will not do willingly, or leave them in the care of a substitute mother. Few can afford competent help, and few can leave young children in someone else's care without feeling guilty about it.

Even when she returns to work to stay, she is at a disadvantage as far as promotion goes. She is presumed not to have the same stability or interest in the job as a man. Her husband's work, not hers, will determine where the family lives, and if his job moves she moves with it. If a child is sick, she and not her husband will take time out from work, and even if no emergency arises she usually has to rush home to prepare dinner.

All these reasons are given by male executives when questioned about opportunities for advancement for women in their firms. But over and above these valid reasons there are others which can be reduced to just plain prejudice—men don't like to take orders from women, women don't think logically, women can't stand the strain of business, certain jobs are men's jobs only. The excellent performance of women workers in all kinds of jobs and even in military services during the war helped to weaken the distinction between "men's jobs" and "women's jobs," but there are still instances where management considers it necessary to rotate men and women in a particular spot lest it become known as a woman's job and the men refuse to do it.

The comforting thought (to men) that nature meant women only for "kinder, kuche, und kirche" can't stand against the obvious fact that nature endowed females with brains as well as hormones. No study has been able to show that women generally are mentally inferior to men; in fact some even indicate that the girls have a slight edge over the boys. The question of whether either sex produces more geniuses or creative minds has no bearing on a discussion of the general population; opportunities and social attitudes are made for and control ordinary people, not geniuses.

The Economic Contribution and Return

In one respect the economic contribution of women is unique—in its flexibility. No matter what the prevailing attitude is toward women's working, in times of

national emergency it becomes their patriotic duty to
man the factories and mind the store while the men are
fighting. Twice in the last fifty years they responded; in
neither case did the number of women working or the
prejudice toward them quite return to the prewar level.

In another, less spectacular, way the flexibility of the
female working force is a boon to industry. Women are
willing to work part-time and at odd hours, an arrangement often beneficial to employer and employee. In the
retail trade, for example, women who cannot or do not
want to work full-time fill in for the rush hours and rush
seasons.

From the long-range viewpoint women form a reser-
voir from which the labor force can be expanded when
the economy requires it. This occurred during the postwar period when the number of women in the labor
force increased by 4 million and the number of men
increased only 3 million. On the other hand, during
periods of recession there is a demand by the men in a
firm to fire the women first, and where the woman is
supplementing rather than supplying the family income
this would cause less hardship and disruption to the
economy.

For many reasons the average earnings of women are
consistently below those of men. Some of the reasons
were cited before—less training, and therefore lower
skills, interrupted work career with loss of seniority,
more part-time work—but after all these have been
allowed for there is still a residual difference which can
be attributed only to traditional prejudice. Women
working at similar duties are sometimes paid less than
men. Frequently, however, the inequity takes the form
of hiring a competent woman at a salary which could

pay only for an incompetent man. This kind of dis-
crimination is difficult to pin down in a survey or to
legislate out of existence.

The principle of equal pay for equal work without
regard to sex is not only a "matter of simple justice," as
President Eisenhower put it, but also serves to protect
the wage scale for the benefit of all workers. It is from
this second point of view that the question has received
most attention, particularly during periods when women
were entering the labor market in large numbers.

During the First World War approximately 3 million
women were suddenly added to the labor force. If the
remaining male workers or the soldiers who were replaced had felt themselves threatened by cheap labor,
it could have meant a serious impairment of morale.
The Bureau of Ordnance of the War Department and
the National War Labor Board both enforced the principle of equal pay for equal work.

During the depression of the 1930's when approximately 3 million women again entered the labor market
in a desperate search for jobs, the equal pay question
again drew official attention. The National Recovery
Administration codes and the Fair Labor Standards Act
of 1938 both established minimum rates, irrespective of
sex.

During the Second World War, almost 6 million
women were added to the labor force. The War, Navy,
and Labor Departments all supported the equal pay
principle, and the National War Labor Board permitted
adjustments in wage rates to equalize pay for women
and men without the approval of the board.

Since that time the problem of equal pay has been a
continuing concern of government, unions, and women's
organizations. By 1956 laws establishing the equal pay

principle for the sexes were in effect in 16 states and
Alaska. Bills to establish the equal pay principle in interstate commerce have been introduced regularly in
Congress since 1945. Pressure for equal and adequate
wages for women will be continuous from now on as
the number of employed women increases steadily.
One-third of our labor force today is women. The other
two-thirds cannot afford the competition of so large a
group if it is underpaid.

An argument to justify a lower rate for women workers, used in a War Labor Board case, is that women work
for pin money, that they are not ordinarily the main
support of a family as a man is, and that therefore they
do not need to earn as much. It is surprising that such
an argument can be seriously advanced in a country
where payment is for work done and not to each according to his need. The only justification for unequal payment is unequal work. If need were to be taken seriously
as a guide in payment, it would have to work both ways.
A company would have to give an increase in salary for
every child born and for every mother-in-law who came
to live with the family.

Income earned by women makes a very substantial
contribution to family income today. In 1954 the median income for families where the wife worked was
$1,300 higher than for families where the wife was not in
the labor force. Only 15 per cent of the families with
nonworking wives had incomes over $7,000 compared
with 27 per cent of the families in which the wife
worked.

This additional income is mostly returned to the economy in the form of consumption—for clothes, personal
maintenance, transportation, and dining out (which become more essential for the working woman), and for

the extras which the family might not otherwise be able
to afford.

Why Work?

Women generally work for the same reason that men
do—because they need money. If this seems an odd
statement to make in this era of high incomes, it must be
remembered that the word "need" has a subjective and
elastic definition. In the pattern of respectability before
the First World War the need for a married woman to
work meant that she was the main support of her family
and had to satisfy the basic need for food and shelter.
This is only partially true today, roughly for about half
of the female working force.

Approximately 25 per cent are listed as family heads
or unrelated individuals, that is, women who do not live
as part of a family group. They obviously need to work
to support themselves. There is another large group,
over 4 million, living with a family but not as a wife—
sister, daughter, mother, etc. These women also must
work to support or help support themselves. Even in
families which are comparatively well off financially,
adult members are usually expected to contribute something toward their maintenance, even a young, unmarried girl if she has finished her schooling. Fifty years
ago the contribution could have been in the form of
household help; today it is more generally expected to
be money. No one questions the right or the need of
these women to gainful employment outside the home,
neither society nor they themselves.

Of the remaining 11.5 million women in the labor
force, approximately 5.7 million are women with children
under 18 years, including 2.2 million who have children

of preschool age. Working mothers of young children, as a group, have been blamed for the rise in juvenile delinquency and have been accused of depriving their young children of essential emotional care, if not physical care. At a Labor Department conference on womanpower, Dr. Leo H. Bartemeier stated:

> It has been evident for some time that a rapidly increasing number of women with small children are trying to span the two worlds of motherhood and careers outside the home. For some, this may be dictated by the necessity of supporting the family, but the much larger number appear to be motivated by neurotic competition. They feel that they must have the luxuries which other women possess. . . .

I would question this statement on the basis of available statistics. The participation of mothers in the labor force is related directly to the husband's income, being greatest when the income is below $4,000, and falling off as income rises. This is hardly a level at which an additional $1,000 a year will provide luxuries. Even at the lower income levels, less than 25 per cent of all women with children under six years old are in the labor force. The presence of young children in the household is such a strong deterrent to the mother working that the proportion in the labor force shows no great difference no matter what group is studied, city, farm, section of the country, educational level, white or nonwhite.

Another important fact is that women with young children seldom hold full-time, year-round jobs. Only two out of ten are likely to be working full-time all year; another four will be working full-time but for only part of the year; the remaining four work part-time.

It is essential to emphasize these statistics because so much emphasis has already been given to the off-to-work movement among all women, even those with very young children, that a rather alarming picture of neglect is created. Whether a woman who leaves her young child in a substitute's care is actually hurting him can only be discussed on an individual basis. The value of a mother's attention and care cannot be graded on the number of hours she spends with her child. Simply being at home does not constitute being a good mother.

More and more women return to work as the children get older and are in school part of the day, needing less constant attention. At any given income level, there is about twice as much chance that the mother will be working if all the children are over six years than if there are any children under six. However, the husband's income is still an important determining factor. Again the largest participation in the work force is in income groups where the father earns less than $4,000 a year, but even when the husband is earning between $7,000 and $10,000, one out of five wives works.

The reasons for working become broader as the children get older. Economic necessity may now include the need to pay for college education for the children, for home improvements long postponed, for a vacation that the family is now grown up enough to take together. It may even mean a simple exchange of one kind of work for another where a woman pays out as much for household help as she earns after taxes.

Just as often it will be the prospect of a future economic need which urges a woman to return to work as soon as she can without disrupting her household. When she reaches 40 she still has an average of 37 years of living to look forward to; her husband, if the same age, can expect to live only 32 years. If he is a couple of years older than she is, the difference in life expectancy may be 8 or 9 years. In other words, if she is realistic she must prepare herself for 8 or 9 years of widowhood.

What are her economic choices for this period if she is not one of the few wealthy widows?

If she has some independent means she may be able to manage by herself by sharply restricting her previous way of living. This is certainly not a choice solution.

If she has children or other accommodating relatives, she may live with them—again not a choice solution. The day of the three-story, three-generation house has passed. Houses and apartments seldom have room easily available for an extra person, and that's what she is likely to remain—an extra rather than an integrated member of the family. Households are small, and household duties are not so great any more that an additional hand can always find work. The family is likely to prize its privacy, and the older woman has learned to prize her independence.

She may consider remarrying, from an economic as well as social viewpoint. Her chances are slim, and she probably knows it. The number of women in the United States begins to exceed the number of men after the age of 25, and the situation gets worse progressively with age. The ratio of 3 widows for every widower has been well advertised.

Her best choice, if she can manage it, is to depend on herself for the major part of her support even if she has her husband's Social Security payments or other small pension. But if she waits much past the age of 40 she will meet increasing resistance to her employment on the grounds of age, particularly if it is her first job after being out of the market for many years. Therefore, at around 35 or 40 years of age, when she can be more easily spared from home duties, she is likely to consider returning to work seriously. It is from this group, married women over 35, that the biggest increase in the labor force has come and will continue to come. In the postwar years there has been an increase of approximately 50 per cent in the number of working wives over 35 years, compared with 10 per cent for wives under 35.

There are compelling reasons, in addition to the economic one, which bring a woman back to work. The feeling that she is wasting her abilities and education crystallizes when she has more time to think about it and the children need her less. Our increasing population and expanding economy have created a continuing need for trained people in many fields including those which are considered women's professions like teaching and nursing. Even for jobs which require less formal education—secretarial work, selling, and clerical work—there are long lists of want advertisements for women. By returning to work, even part-time, a woman with older children can fill an economic need in her community, supplement her income, and have the satisfaction of using skills which she may have put into moth balls ten or fifteen years before.

At every income level the proportion of working wives increases as the education of the wife increases. In families where the husband is earning between $7,000 and $10,000 one-quarter of the wives who have four or more years of college are working. Even when the husband earns more than $10,000, about 18 per cent of the wives who have completed college are working.

One other need is important in bringing women back to work when the children are in school—the need for emotional independence, the need to provide interests and duties to replace mothering when that job is done. Increasing life expectancy has made this not a matter of a few declining years but rather a substantial period of perhaps twenty or twenty-five active years. Women have heard often enough by now that they must not hang on to their mature children, and few relish the idea of becoming an interfering mother-in-law or a devouring grandmother. For her own sake, as well as her children's, a woman must avoid the emptiness which can come with the end of active motherhood, and the depression which often accompanies the feeling of uselessness.

Working is the best solution for many, particularly when part-time jobs are available to supplement what is becoming for her a part-time job at home. If she is widowed in later years, the job will be an emotional as well as an economic resource for her.

These are the reasons women want to work. The growing economy and the multiplying population, which have a very real need for their services, made it possible for them to work. They provided the opportunity and eroded the walls of prejudice, so that women could not only reenter the business world in large numbers but could also get into jobs which were practically closed to them before the war.

The development of mechanical servants and partially processed foods have made it easier for women to work outside the home but have not provided the opportunity or the incentive. The same is true for birth control, which makes it possible for a woman to say with some assurance, at a relatively early age, that she has completed one cycle of her life and is ready to start the next.

What of the Future?

There is no question that the number of women in the labor force will continue high and even increase in the foreseeable future. The basic reasons for the increase and the opportunity provided by an expanding economy will continue important. More and more women will feel the need of some long-term career, although for the majority it will continue to be limited by family requirements. For most women their work will remain supplementary and secondary to their husband's work.

The kind of jobs held by women will be upgraded by automation, which will eliminate much of the routine and detail work they now perform. This is particularly true of clerical work in banks and insurance companies, which are today so swamped with paper work that they are excellent prospects for computers. In the long run this will not mean unemployment for women workers, but absorption into jobs requiring higher skills and more training.

Women are already being called upon to train for technological work, even in areas formerly considered a man's job, for there is an unfilled national need for these skills. Signs of the times can be found in advertisements —a girl advertising a sweater is posed working in a laboratory—and in television programs, which carefully include at least one female worker in laboratory settings, even on missile programs. In addition, the knowledge that the majority of Russian doctors are women will encourage us to make more use of a relatively untapped source of brain power.

The ideal solution to the problem of prejudice against women in industry and science is, of course, the same as the solution to the problem of any kind of prejudice, to judge each individual according to his or her ability and performance and only on that basis. If nine out of ten women cannot measure up in a particular line of work, say engineering, then on that basis alone they will not compete successfully. The tenth may be an excellent engineer, and it should be her right to be one without being labeled aggressive, unfeminine, neurotic. If nine out of ten women prefer to give up any chance of advancement by staying at home for a period of years, or permanently, this should not affect the chances of the tenth who chooses to remain in the business world.

Additional educational opportunities for women wishing to return to the business or professional world would benefit the women and the industries which need their services. Refresher or special training courses could be designed for women who have been at home for a number of years and perhaps still cannot leave home full-time for training. Such courses, for example, might be concentrated in the hours when children are in school or in the evenings when husbands are home and can take over. This is already being done successfully in the teaching field, where the shortage is acute. One program, under a grant from the Ford Foundation, gives financial aid to qualified applicants to help them take a concentrated teacher-training program.

Community Participation

Early in the history of the United States, after the Civil War, women started to organize clubs as one means of enlarging their horizons. The early ones were devoted to culture and self-improvement activities like book clubs, lectures, and bird watching. Although this movement had some value in opening the doors to out-

of-home activities for women within an acceptable
framework, the movement has continued strong even to
current times, when action on problems is essential
rather than lectures and discussions alone.

To some extent women who wish to participate actively in community affairs, and particularly in politics,
are discouraged by their own feeling that they may be
neglecting their duties at home for a nonessential activity and the still prevalent idea that politics is a dirty
business and therefore not suitable for a woman. Both
these attitudes must be dispelled. We have a desperate
need for a politically mature citizenry today, and
women form more than half the voting population of
this country.

It is strange that when a woman undertakes civic activities on a volunteer basis, she may be condemned for
expecting her family to make some adjustment in sched-
ule, for leaving her husband with the children, for cooking or baking less elaborately. Even today it is assumed
that her first, and preferably her only, allegiance is to
her family, particularly if the alternative is civic participation rather than paid employment. In the latter, there
is an obvious monetary return to the family for giving
up part of the mother's time.

The return to the family from the mother's participation in the affairs and politics of the community should
also be recognized, even if it is less obvious than a salary.
Until it is, we will be wasting the energies and abilities
of many women who could spare some time from home
duties but do not need to, or are not ready to, work.

As in the business world, women are found in largest
numbers in the lower echelons in politics. As in the
business world, individual women have reached high
posts, as high as the cabinet and senate, but for the most

part they do the leg work rather than make the policy
decisions. In organizations of their own, however, outside the political parties, women have accomplished
some spectacular results, which should be given wider
publicity.

- Achieving permanent registration in many
states.
- Extension of civil service in many states.
- Passage of the Pure Food and Drug Law.
- Revision of the Missouri state constitution.
- Revision of the pardon system in Georgia.
- Securing laws to establish county and district
health units in Nebraska.
- Passage of a school attendance law in Ohio.
- Passage of a modern milk code in Boulder,
Colorado.

The list is representative but by no means complete.
The record of accomplishments could be longer and
more impressive if the community recognized the urgent
need for the part-time participation of its women in its
government, encouraged such participation, and publicized its achievements. It is not necessary for a woman
to make a career out of politics in order to contribute to
her community. She can serve a special function within
a restricted area if she has little time or cannot go far,
ringing doorbells to get out the voters, distributing literature, bringing issues to the attention of her neighbors.
The issues may be local, national, or international. They
may concern an ineffective school board officer, a state
primary contest, or nuclear testing. As a citizen, she
must be concerned with all.

Overestimating the Power of a Woman

The accusation has been made and often repeated that American women own, operate, control, and dominate the American economy and the American male. Statistics are quoted to prove the point, some reliable, some based on an isolated survey, some in the "it-is-estimated" class, but frequently with a scandalized air, as if this marked the beginning of the decline and fall of Western civilization.

Let us start with the economy and emphasize first that there is a distinction between owning and controlling, between paying bills and incurring them, between actually making a purchase and deciding what to buy.

Women own 52 per cent of all common stocks listed. If this gives a picture of 56 million American women each with a little bundle of stocks in her name, dismiss it. The bulk is still owned by a few wealthy women, although there are more and more middle-income women being added to the list of stockholders. This is perhaps the best place to emphasize that owning is not necessarily controlling. Women generally leave their investment decisions to men, and prefer men as stock brokers. They do not control companies they "own" (companies in which women own more than 50 per cent of the stock include some of the giants of industry—A. T. & T., du Pont, and General Electric). Women are seldom found on the board of directors or in high executive posts; they have little voice in determining policy within the company. They probably invested for dividend checks, and if the stock is safe and pays as expected they are satisfied.

Women own approximately half, or perhaps slightly more, of all savings accounts and government bonds.

Women also constitute more than half of the adult population. Why then should proportionate ownership be startling unless it is assumed that women have no ownership rights?

Women handle the money and pay the bills in 38 per cent of all American families; in another 31 per cent of the families the husband and wife together handle the money and pay the bills. This leaves 31 per cent of the families with the men paying the bills and handling the money, according to a University of Michigan study. If we break the 31 per cent for joint handling in half, we come out with nearly a 50–50 relationship for the handling of money and paying bills in the United States.

These figures can only be alarming if we start out by agreeing with the Koran that women stand inferior to men. In addition, paying a bill has nothing to do with incurring the debt. A woman may actually write the checks on the first of the month because she has more time or wishes to save her husband the trouble. If she pays a gasoline bill that he has run up during the month or a mortgage installment on the house that they decided to buy jointly, she can hardly be said to control the money.

Women buy or influence the purchase of 60 to 85 per cent of all goods and services in the United States. No one really knows what the figure is, but these are the limits of the most-often-quoted estimates. Such estimates and the surveys on which they are based are the legitimate concern of the advertising agencies, which must, as a part of their operation, know who buys what and why. But as proof of the hold of the American woman on the economy, they should be taken with a shaker full of salt.

Actually buying and deciding what to buy are two

different things. A woman buys many family items like food as part of her housekeeping job. No doubt this is one part of the market she dominates, but even here she is influenced to some extent by her husband's preferences and by which premium junior wants with his cereal. She buys most of her own clothes, but how many dresses are returned because her husband didn't like them? She may even buy his shirts and socks, but, if he picked the brand, style, and color before she went to the store, to whom should the purchase be attributed? When a house is bought or a vacation arranged, does it matter who puts down the deposit when the purchase has been preceded by weeks of joint planning?

With more and more women working, and with men spending more time at home, it is probable that women's influence over buying will increase while their actual purchasing may decrease. The last stronghold of the American female—the supermarket—has already been heavily invaded by men. Today a woman on a week-end shopping trip not only must compete against other housewives, but also is likely to find her access to the potatoes barred by a strapping six-foot male.

Women owned 60 billion dollars worth of life insurance in 1956. This figure has been quoted by itself more than once and sounds enormous. The complete statement, however, is that women own 60 billion dollars worth of life insurance, about 15 per cent of the total in force in the United States. Women receive approximately 75 per cent of all life-insurance death benefits, 60 per cent as wives and the remainder in other relationships.

There are two reasons why women are the main inheritors of wealth in this country. First, women have been less able to support themselves and have had to be provided for. Second, and growing more important, is that women, on the average, live longer than men and are alive to inherit what men leave. The present difference in life expectancy is a little over six years more for women, a difference growing more pronounced year by year.

Since one of the leading causes of excess male mortality is heart disease, there has been built up an unfortunately popular notion that greedy, lazy American wives drive their husbands to an early grave with overwork to supply them with furs and jewels. If this is true, American women start pretty early; there is an excess male mortality even before the beginning of life (stillbirths), through infancy, childhood, and adulthood.

The widening difference in mortality rates is due to the shift from communicable diseases to degenerative diseases as a cause of death, and the sharp decline in the maternity death rate. It should be noted, particularly by foreign observers who are so fond of berating the selfish American wife that, in the words of the Health Information Foundation, "Excess male mortality is by no means peculiar to the United States. Rather, it is common, with only minor exceptions, throughout much of the world. In general, the differential is greatest where life expectancy is highest, and widens as each country's mortality rate declines."

Scientists are not yet prepared to say to what extent environmental factors account for the mortality difference, but few doubt that there is some relationship. Women, for example, consult physicians more regularly than men, probably because of the economic pressure which keeps a man on the job. (He may also be afraid of being thought a sissy.) Men may be subject to more internal strains and pressure because they hold more important jobs in industry and government. There is no simple answer to the disparity in mortality rates. If it results in making American women pretty rich, it also leaves them very lonely.

Where Is the Pedestal?

Where is the overprivileged, pampered, useless parasite that is supposed to be representative of American women? No doubt she exists, but to extend this picture to 56 million women, most of whom drive themselves instead of their husbands, is inaccurate and unfair. There are many more women standing on subways or buses on the way to work than on pedestals being worshipped.

Women drive themselves in an attempt to be a combination mother (which includes den-mother, chauffeur, supervisor-of-the-homework, nurse, P.T.A. participant), community worker, and career girl, and with it all to remain a glamour girl. Here the double standard operates again. Gray hair at the temples is romantic only in men; in women it is a sign of criminal neglect.

With some change in society's values, women could perform whatever function suits them best without feeling inferior or insecure in their choice. Ideally, the woman who never marries but follows a useful line of work should be able to feel on a par with the mother of six children who never earns a cent in her life, or the woman who does both at appropriate times in her life, or the woman who devotes her time to volunteer rather than paid employment.

We are a long way from such an ideal, and the recurring cries of matriarchy will not advance us toward it.

Women are not deserting their biologic and traditional role in the home, and there is no sign that they want to. The birth rate is high, and the home is the new center

of activity. Instead, they are trying to add to their traditional role, and a society as troubled as today's needs
whatever talents it can get. Let us take from our women
any contribution they can make in whatever areas they
can best contribute, giving recognition to unpaid work
in the home and the community. The trade in tranquiliz-
ers may suffer, but women and society in general will
profit.

AUTOMATION

3

Of Machines and Men

Automation is a widely used, ill-defined term, the subject of union policies, management conferences, and congressional hearings. It is minimized as just another step in the long history of mechanization, or hailed as the second industrial revolution. To some it is the promise of utopia with a six and one-half day weekend; to others it foreshadows a terrible depression. It is said to have begun with the invention of the cave man's club or with the invention of the vacuum tube. It is a word used with emotional overtones of wonder or fear, the concrete fear of losing a job to a machine and the more nebulous fear of a science-fiction world dominated by "thinking machines." If we have become oversophisticated and generally incapable of wonder, our reaction to automation's machinery is an exception. The causes for wonder increase with each new automation development.

- One machine, for example, weighs the ingredients for bread, mixes them just the required amount, puts the dough in loaf form in the oven, takes it out when baked, slices and wraps each loaf, and delivers it to the loading platform almost without human intervention.
- A machine sorts and measures connecting rods in an automobile plant so exactly that all that go into one engine are identical.
- Another machine records and analyzes stock data from scattered branches and then prints reports indicating where and when replacement will be necessary.
- There is a machine that takes orders from a punched tape and produces a master cam for a plane engine in 40 hours instead of 300.
- Still another machine with electronic controls produces a superior defraction grating with tolerances held to incredibly small limits.
- But one of the few things these machines cannot do is think!

At the Congressional hearings on automation in 1955 these two opposing statements were made.

First: "Now, through automation . . . and I think this is perhaps the basic meaning of automation . . . we are beginning to look at our industrial processes as complete, integrated systems, from the introduction of the raw material until the completion of the final product."

The second statement: "Automation comes in bits and pieces. First the automating of a single process, and then gradually a tying together of several processes to get a group or subassembly complete."

The first point of view emphasizes integration of all processes and would tend to break down the dividing lines between material handling and production, between different phases of production, and between office and factory. In many cases it would necessitate redesigning a product to make more complete integration possible. The second viewpoint is closer to current practice, at least in the mass production industries where manufacturing is divisible.

In considering the economic consequences of automation we must include both approaches. In the long run, however, the view of production as an integrated unit is likely to prevail. Mechanization broke production into separate units which are finally assembled. Automation will tend to reverse this trend.

If automation is just another step in the continuing process of replacing human labor with machines, it is certainly a giant step. New elements have been added which make the change qualitative rather than just quantitative. When a man operates a machine, the speed of the process is limited by human abilities. When the operator is no longer needed, the speed of the process is limited only by the speed of the machine. For example, electronic computers do their adding and subtracting with the speed of light. Each action is accomplished within 20 millionths of a second. Electronic engineers are even considering a new unit of time based on the speed of light—a light-foot, or the time it takes light to travel one foot at the rate of 186,000 miles a second.

In addition, the machine has begun to perform, on a large scale, functions until recently considered uniquely human—functions of the brain and the sense organs. Electronic equipment can see, hear, taste, touch, and smell. Through their sense organs the machines can communicate and control other machines.

The aim of current research is to organize production into closed systems, where sensing devices gather information, computers analyze it and feed orders to other devices which actuate the machine tools. This closed system underlies the concept of a "push-button" factory. It does not imply, however, that the factory will not need people to run it. The fewer production workers that are needed, the more engineers and maintenance men will be required to keep the machinery going.

Automation Defined

Although a precise definition of automation, in the dictionary sense, is not possible and not even essential, we must understand what we are discussing if we are to make any valid estimate of the economic effects. The technological advances which fall within the broadest definition of automation can be divided into three groups for convenience. The second and third are the new features of automation.

First, there is the use of more automatic machinery, particularly "transfer machines" which carry the workpiece from one machine tool to another. Thus, a series of operations which were formerly considered separate become part of a continuous production line. One of the best examples is the Ford engine plant in Cleveland. In fact, the word automation was coined by a Ford executive in connection with just this type of machinery, and it has since been labeled "Detroit automation."

Second, there is the use of feedback devices or servomechanisms which act as sense organs to check the performance of the machine, compare it with pre-set requirement for the product, and correct the process if necessary. It is frequently pointed out that the concept of a self-regulating machine is not new, that it goes back to Roman days and is exemplified in the governor on Watt's steam engine and the ordinary room thermostat. As a concept it may not be new, but as a reality applied to industrial production it is very new.

Research started in the 1930's but was sharply accelerated during the war when the speed with which a gun was aimed had to match the speed of the plane it was shooting at. Gun-laying became automatic, with a speed and accuracy impossible to a human operator. When the war ended, the Massachusetts Institute of Technology Servomechanisms Laboratory undertook research aimed at utilizing industrially the principles developed during the war.

The greatest progress in the use of these devices has thus far been in continuous process industries, that is, those in which the production process must be carried through completely without stopping, as, for example, chemicals, plastics, and synthetic fibers.

The third feature is the introduction of general and special-purpose computing machines to record, store, and analyze information. These are the machines which, with little human help, produce the Sears Roebuck payroll, keep track of all the check accounts in a bank, or decide which bids to accept in a complicated situation. Again the new computers may be said to be simply an extension of earlier data-processing machines, but the addition of a "memory" and their extraordinary speed put them into a different class for practical purposes. In one second a modern data-processing machine can "read" instructions and go through several thousand steps (addition, subtraction, etc.), print the results, even draw a graph, and during the process distinguish exceptions to routine procedure. The degree of accuracy is also incredible, and errors are corrected by the machine itself.

When properly instructed, a computer can do "accounting by exception." This means that given a mass of data to process, it can choose the cases which deviate from normal or which require special attention instead of printing all results. Thus, in the case where the machine keeps track of the stock status of a larger number of parts, it will print reports only when the stock is low, is concentrated in the wrong branch, is in surplus supply, was ordered but didn't come, etc. In deciding whether to print a report for a given item the machine takes account of such factors as the time it takes to get the part and the number used during the past few months.

What Automation Can Accomplish

What industry can hope to achieve through the use of these new machines is the fullest, most efficient use of all its resources, human, raw material, and machine. To think of automation purely as a labor-saving device is to overlook its greatest economic potentials. It will certainly cut down on the labor required wherever it is applied, but it will also enable industry to supply more consumer goods at lower prices by increasing productivity. Increasing production has been the basis for the rising standard of living throughout our history; automation will give it new impetus.

Automation control over production can cut waste to a negligible factor by keeping production continually at an optimum level. For example, it has been estimated that a first rate petroleum refinery operates at peak performance for only a few minutes out of a 24-hour day. Blending is used at the end of the production process to bring the product up to standard. However, in industries where the product is not a mixture and cannot be blended, there is a high percentage of waste. Plastics like polyethylene and synthetic fibers are either right or wrong. If wrong they go into waste and increase the cost of the right part to the consumer.

Automation equipment will perform tasks previously impossible or impractical. The whole atomic energy industry could not exist without distant automatic controls to handle the radioactive materials. The ultra-precision required in some manufacturing processes today, with tolerances limited to a few millionths of an inch, would not be possible without the electronic devices which not only measure but frequently correct errors as they occur.

In the field of data processing the possibilities are just being realized. Firms that bought electronic "brains" to do accounting are finding their real value lies not so much in direct dollar savings but indirectly in the performance of analytical work which before would have been prohibitively time consuming. The machine can work out the results of alternative courses of action, thus taking the guesswork out of decisions.

Several examples will serve to illustrate this potential. A major airline used a computer to decide how to reroute its planes in case of a breakdown. There were thousands of possible solutions, in fact, so many that it was impossible, without the computer, to work them all out and choose the best. The company was forced to keep standby planes unused to provide for the emergency. However, the computer worked out all the possible solutions in a matter of hours, was able to indicate the best, and the company saved a million dollars a year formerly lost in revenues while the planes stood idle.

General Electric uses its UNIVAC not only for the routine jobs of billing, payroll, and cost accounting but in coordinating sales reports from the field with production schedules, for factory scheduling, and product development. The Bureau of the Census has found that the use of a computer not only cut the cost of the population survey in half but also enabled the Bureau to perform statistical tasks previously impossible because of the cost.

With a computer, business decisions can be made on the basis of more complete, accurate, and recent data, analyzed according to management's needs. So important can such data be that Sylvania Electric is using a nationwide 20,000-mile private electronic communications system to link 88 company locations with the data-processing center outside of Syracuse.

Economic Effects

No one seriously advocates that we try to halt or slow down automation because of the economic dislocation it may produce. Technological progress is now too much a part of American life for any one to yell the equivalent of "Get a horse!" On the other hand, automation must not be pictured as a relentless fog slowly enveloping American industry on its own momentum. Management will automate only when it finds it profitable to do so because of direct and indirect savings.

Automation is not a cheap procedure, and business must have a strong economic motive for undertaking it.

For example, if the market for a product can be substantially expanded by lowering the price, and if automation can accomplish this required price reduction, the change might be undertaken. Or if the quality of a product is not satisfactory and could be greatly improved by electronic monitoring, there might be sufficient motive for introducing automation. Or when a firm simply cannot handle its potential volume with the existing machinery setup or available labor, automation might be economically justifiable.

One need, in addition to the economic one, will encourage the progress of automation—the need to maintain our pre-eminence in productivity as part of national defense. If we cannot afford to let the U.S.S.R. outstrip us in the missile program or graduate more engineers and scientists, we certainly cannot afford to be second best in our production methods. The launching of the Sputniks destroyed the last of the ostriches who were happy in the belief that Russian technology was at least fifty years behind ours, and that any advances that were made were on the basis of secrets stolen from the United States.

In general, all segments of the economy welcome progress, change, and the increasing productivity which automation promises. Probably the most positive attitude toward automation by a labor union is shown by the action of the Amalgamated Lithographers of America. This group has proposed a 2 million dollar union-management fund to promote automation in the industry and has appointed a director of technology to work with management in studying new machinery and procedures in order to bring them into the industry quickly and beneficially.

However, many unions add an "if" to their optimism.

Take for example the statement of Walter P. Reuther, made before a Congressional committee. "First of all, we fully realize that the potential benefits of automation are great, if properly handled." It is such "ifs" which prompted the inquiry by Congress into the nature and implications of automation, the extent of potential employment displacement, the need for training and retraining displaced workers, and the distribution of anticipated gains in productivity.

For there is fear among workers of displacement and downgrading. It is widespread enough to have reached the comics, and a public opinion poll in Detroit showed that what the majority feared most next to Russia was automation. How far such fear can go is illustrated by a bitter strike in the Standard Motors plant in England, which was attributed to company plans to install automatic machinery.

To what extent is this fear justified? Among the most encouraging signs that gross errors will be avoided is the wide public recognition given to the problem and the realization that its solution is a joint responsibility. One of the conclusions of the Congressional inquiry was that while "only a relatively small . . . fraction of the total labor force will be directly involved . . . no one dare overlook or deny that many individuals will suffer mental and physical hardships as adjustments go forward." To this should be added the statement made on behalf of the Labor Department "that the human values must not be overlooked or underestimated, that there should be consultation with workers."

In studying the probable effects of automation on labor, there are two kinds of displacement to be considered—the worker who is displaced by a new machine and the worker who is not hired because of the new machine. The first is the more immediate problem, and the unions argue that solutions must be worked out jointly with the financial burden borne by management. George Meany put it this way, "the collective bargaining process must be utilized to work out the necessary arrangement for introducing the new machinery and equipment, for reviewing the wage structure and job classification. . . ."

The United Automobile Workers (UAW) has made it a policy to include clauses in their contracts providing for the training and retraining at company expense of workers who must master new skills and getting companies to raise the age limit on apprenticeships so that older unskilled and semiskilled men could enter the programs. In a plan worked out with the Ford Company in the spring of 1957, the company agreed to remove the former age limit of 26 for apprentices and permit any seniority employee who goes into the apprenticeship program to take related classroom instruction at company expense.

Automation has not progressed far enough for the effects to be detectable in national labor statistics. The fragmentary reports available thus far do not show large-scale layoffs. Economic dislocations which do occur will tend to be concentrated in a particular industry or area and can be a serious problem locally without denting the national economy.

Case Histories

For an estimate of the problems arising when a company introduces some phase of automation we must rely, at this stage, on the case studies presented in detail by the Labor Department. The following three cases represent three different types of operations, a mass-production factory, a continuous-production industry, and a data-processing company. They all have this in common—the introduction of new technologies was accomplished with a minimum of hardship and dislocation.

The first company manufactured radio, phonograph, and television sets, using purchased, standard components. Conventional methods of assembly involved the handling of several hundred parts and soldered connections.

The new technology consisted of the introduction of printed circuits to replace the conventional, soldered wire connections. In this case, the product was redesigned instead of using an automatic machine to do just what previously was done by hand. The change was made when new models were being introduced, and union officials were informed two weeks in advance of the action.

There was no net effect on the number of people employed. Some unskilled jobs were eliminated; in this case they were jobs held mostly by women. New machine-tending jobs were created for which the company gave previous employees two weeks' training. Other semiskilled and skilled jobs were created, including an industrial engineering staff. As far as possible, old employees were transferred to new jobs, and where this was not possbile they were transferred to other parts of the factory. The pay rates for automated jobs were set 5 to 15 per cent above the previous rates for unskilled labor. The change was accomplished during a period of expanding production and employment.

The second company, a bakery, undertook a more extensive change over a longer period. It involved the building of a new factory, and the complete procedure took five years. During the entire time, there were frequent conferences with the union, and a new contract was negotiated which considerably lessened the impact the change might have had. The contract provided for changes in scheduled hours which cut the necessary reduction in employment by an estimated 25 per cent. It also provided that workers shifted to less skilled jobs would not take a cut in pay.

In the new factory, separate facilities were combined into a single unit. The bread-making process was so integrated that, except for one stage, no manual handling was required from receipt of dry ingredients to the finished loaf at the loading platform.

During the first full year of operation there were some layoffs, but output expanded, and two years later the total number employed for production was slightly higher than before the change. Previous employees were retrained for new jobs where possible, and, where they could not adapt themselves, they were given other jobs at the same pay rate. In general, the new jobs required greater responsibility and less physical labor.

The consensus among the workers was that on the whole the change was advantageous. For management, it meant that productivity was multiplied forty times, and there was a reduction in the loss due to waste and spoilage.

The third case is a life insurance company whose operation requires rapid and accurate processing of a constantly increasing, routine paperwork. For fifteen years the company had been plagued by a labor shortage. The clerical staff included a high proportion of recent high school graduates, and there was a complete labor turnover every five years.

The installation of a large electronic computer in one section resulted in a reduction of approximately 50 per cent in the budget for that section. The work could be handled by 21 punch card machines and 85 employees instead of 125 machines and 198 employees. The new setup took 15,000 feet less floor space. The average salary per employee in the section increased from $3,700 to $4,200. The company expected its actual investment to be returned in direct savings in 4 years.

The employees were notified in advance of the intended installation and kept informed on progress and prospects. They were carefully interviewed for job preference in other sections and possible retraining for jobs on the computer staff. One electronics engineer was brought in from the outside; the remainder of the computer staff was selected from the company's employees and trained for the new jobs. There were no discharges or downgrading.

Three factors contributed to the success of the installation from the viewpoint of labor adjustment: there were similar jobs in other divisions, the company was growing, and it always had a high labor turnover, which meant that instead of firing they just didn't hire replacements for people who left. The worker who was displaced was the next June's graduate.

It should be noted that these three dissimilar installations had one important circumstance in common which made it possible to avoid discharges and to keep layoffs to a minimum. All three companies were in a growth phase and could transfer displaced personnel to different jobs within the organization.

On a national scale, it will also be true that if the economy continues to expand, the workers who are not hired in the automated industries will be absorbed in other sections of the economy. During periods of recession there is normally a slowdown in capital goods investment. Since automation requires heavy capital goods expenditures, it will make least progress during periods of economic weakness and most progress during prosperous years when displaced workers are most easily absorbed.

Minimizing Hardship

One problem which did not arise in these three companies will have to be faced as automation spreads. It is frequently more economical for a company to build a new plant than to rebuild an old one, particularly in factories where integration of processes is a prime objective, as in the case of the bakery. Since the relative importance of labor in production is cut sharply by advanced automation, there is less need to build the factory in or near large labor centers. Although the company may bear the financial burden of moving the employees with the factory, there are many ties which may keep the worker in his established home. This is particularly true for older people.

Some shock absorbers—like state unemployment benefits—exist now, but pressure will increase for industry to grant substantial severance pay, and supplementary unemployment benefits, and to adjust pension plans to permit earlier retirement in such cases. These methods may also be used, generally, to alleviate the hardship of the older worker who cannot be fitted into the new scheme.

Thus the hardship resulting from the introduction of

automation machinery can be kept at a minimum, although not eliminated, by the assumption of responsibility by all sections of the economy, by working out new wage scales and schedules jointly, by training programs and special help in finding new jobs, and by financial benefits during temporary layoffs.

These are all measures which have proved themselves possible and effective for immediate needs, and there is always time to work them out equitably. For one characteristic of a switch to automation which is on the side of adjustment is the fact that it takes time . . . not weeks, but months or years. There is time for training programs to be planned and carried out, and there is time for consultation and spreading information. During this interim period, the labor force can be sometimes reduced by attrition, with only temporary employees hired to replace those who leave, or retirements postponed to make replacements unnecessary.

In the long run, however, the worker who is not hired rather than the one who is fired will present the challenge to our economy. After 1960 we should begin to see the effects on the labor force of the high birth rate during and after the Second World War. The increase will be only partly offset by the additional years devoted to education and by earlier retirement. Two well-established procedures, rather than new techniques, must be depended on to accomplish the absorption of these workers. These are the reduction in the work week and the expansion of the economy with a rising standard of living.

Organized labor has already begun its campaign for a shorter week with no reduction in pay. Union leaders argue that rising productivity will force the four-day week on industry if wide unemployment is to be avoided. But if the purchasing power is reduced, there will be no market even for the output of a four-day week.

Most important in the long-range adjustment prospects will be our ability to keep the economy dynamic, to keep our purchasing power at the point where the consumer can absorb the bigger and better products of automation. There is no imminent saturation point for the needs, or rather the desires, of the American consumer. Historically, we have always been anxious to buy new products and more old ones which could add to comfort or social standing. Today it is invention that mothers necessity rather than the traditional converse. Discretionary purchasing will have to expand again.

Who can say what new products and processes will come out of the laboratory and off the drawing board tomorrow to give new impetus to the economy as television, frozen foods, and plastics did yesterday? But they will come, and they will absorb some part of the labor force. Science and invention have always stimulated industrial production and consumer spending.

The electronics industry itself is an illustration. Sales of electronic equipment and replacement parts for 1958 are expected to reach more than 8 billion dollars. Sales of industrial and commercial electronic equipment alone (excluding military, replacement, and consumer) will reach an estimated 1.5 billion dollars.

This is still an infant industry. One of the earliest purchases of a UNIVAC was by the Bureau of the Census in 1950, and the first industrial installation came four years later. In the following two years manufacturers shipped approximately 1,200 stored-program computers. Demand for computers is currently outstripping supply, and manufacturers are increasing present capacities or building new plants.

It has been argued that the electronics industry, being highly automated itself, will not require many people, but it must be remembered that, in addition to those engaged in actual production, the men who design, sell, install, and maintain the equipment, hold jobs that did not exist ten years ago. Other industries, still in their infancy or yet unborn, will arise only because of technological progress and will also absorb their quota of the labor force. How many? We cannot possibly estimate nor should we attempt to set limits, but, for an idea of the potential, note that the number of people employed in the chemical and allied industries exceeds the number employed in all forms of mining, including coal, metals, petroleum, and natural gas.

Lower prices, made possible by advancing technology, will be another growth factor in the future economy, as they have been in the past. The car would never have become a part of standard equipment for the American family without assembly line production, and television could not have become a national pastime without the automatic machinery used in manufacturing it.

In many industries the decline in employment because of the use of automation machinery will be more than offset by the increase because of expanding production. Telecommunications, which pioneered in the use of automatic machinery, showed an employment gain of 75 per cent between 1940 and 1950, the highest for any group of major industries except public administration. Since the end of the war, chemicals, instrument manufacture, and electrical machinery, all industries in which automation has made progress, have shown larger than average per cent increases in employment.

"Side Effects" of Automation

What will be the effects on the labor force aside from actual employment or unemployment? What of working conditions, the kind of skills required, the distribution of labor among different industries?

There will be a shift of employment away from manufacturing to the service industries. These industries are less suited to automation, and productivity cannot be increased at the same rate as in manufacturing. In addition, there will be an increased need and desire for services of all kinds. The industries which cater to leisure activities will have an expanding market as the workweek is shortened, vacations are extended, and the number of holidays is increased. The marketing services, selling, advertising, and promotion, will be needed to stimulate consumer purchasing so that no gap develops between production and consumption. Educational services will have to expand to meet industry's need for trained personnel and the human need for knowledge and judgment in a complex world.

Working conditions will be greatly improved by the elimination of physical hazards in factories. A worker stationed at control panels at a distance from the actual production process will not be subjected to conditions of heat, humidity, ventilation, and noise which are necessary for the product but may be harmful to him. Since the worker will seldom actually handle the machine, and since manual handling of heavy materials will be eliminated, the possibility of accidents and physical strain will be eliminated to the same degree. The working environment will be safer and healthier.

The changes in skill requirements under automation

will be away from unskilled and semiskilled jobs, to those requiring more skill and more judgment. There will be an increased need for electronic engineers, maintenance personnel, and for highly trained people to program the machines. (This really means setting up the machine so that it will do the work required.)

In a study made by the University of Michigan's Survey Research Center on two plants of the Detroit Edison Company, one automated and one conventional, it was found that all the men in the new plant were more interested in their new jobs than they had been in their former jobs at the old plant. They felt that the broadened jobs utilized their abilities and reduced the monotony of the work. This case demonstrates the fact that automation will reverse a trend set up by mechanization. When industry mechanized it created many specialized, routine, and monotonous jobs. When it automates this is the kind of work which will be eliminated.

The Department of Labor estimates that by 1965 the proportion of white-collar workers (professional, proprietors and managers, clerical and sales) will reach 42 per cent of total employment, and will for the first time exceed the proportion of blue-collar workers (craftsmen, operatives, laborers). By 1975 professional personnel may account for approximately 12 per cent of the labor force compared with about 10 per cent today.

Automation and computers in particular will put a premium on good management. The decision whether to automate production or to buy a computer is a far-reaching one, and in the process of making the decision problems will be uncovered which have never been recognized as problems. If it is decided that a computer is justified, reorganization must be undertaken. This frequently includes the physical reorganization of departments, for a computer is not simply a substitute for another type of machine.

With a computer, tighter statistical control will be possible, and quick decisions will be essential. With the mountain of paperwork reduced perhaps to a hill, top management will spend more time on policy making, and the standards of good management will go up— much as the Saturday night bath became a daily routine when it was no longer necessary to pump water. Management also will have the task of formulating the problems that the computer is to solve, and this will have to be done in the most precise manner. The computer has neither judgment nor flexibility, and will follow only exact instructions.

The director of a computer section will not have to be a computer expert but he will have to know enough to understand the capability of the machine, and whether the problem, as translated into computer language, represents what he wants to know. Nor will he have to be an electronics engineer, but if he is to deal with scientists extensively he would do well to understand their jargon.

There will be a new kind of labor-relations problem, at first in adjusting to a new setup with a minimum of disruption to the firm and employees and later in securing and holding the necessary force of computer experts. In the present early stage of automation many companies are training their own employees for the computer staff, but eventually the universities will have to take over this job and the companies will hire trained personnel. Unlike the specialist in other fields the computer expert will be concerned only with how to solve a problem, and it will make no difference to him whether the data concern petticoats or petroleum. He will be able to shift easily from one company to another, and management will have to find incentives peculiarly attractive to this group.

Second only to the wide concern over possible employment dislocations is the question of the competitive position of small business under automation. What of the small and medium-sized company that produces in short runs and doesn't need and cannot afford the specialized machinery which typifies "Detroit automation," or a giant "brain?"

The assumption that a company must be prepared to invest nearly a million dollars or to produce its product in exceptionally long runs in order to use automatic equipment is not entirely true now and will be less so in the future. A small company may have good use for a computer but not need a UNIVAC. To meet this need, a number of computer manufacturers are designing smaller, general-purpose models. Several already available sell for around $40,000; one can be rented for about $1,000 a month. The practice of renting machines, widespread among computer manufacturers, will be a great help to smaller firms who cannot make a substantial capital investment. It is even possible to rent time on a computer when the amount of work needed is too small to justify renting a machine. Universities, in particular, rent time on their computers.

A recent automation development promises to be important for the estimated 80 per cent of industry that produces in small lots rather than in mass production runs. This is the tape-controlled machine tool which takes its instructions from a magnetic or punched tape. These machines are based on the feedback principle, and changing the production run is only a matter of changing the tape. Use of such machines would allow the job-shop producer to take advantage of automation and still retain his traditional advantage, flexibility.

The intensive development of these machines may well be the important trend in automation in the next few years. Their natural field will be missiles, electronics, aircraft, in fact, any industry where engineering changes are so rapid and production runs so small that it is economically impossible to set up a "Detroit automation" production line. Since production specifications are fed directly to the machine in the form of punched tape, the detailed drawings and specifications which the human operator needed are eliminated, as is much of the retooling formerly necessary. In addition, the speed of the machines cuts down on the inventory requirements.

A significant advance is the new Digitape electronic control system installed at the Hughes aircraft plant for production of electronic systems for the government. In this system one tape controls the machines which mill, drill, and bore the part being machined, and transfer the workpiece from one machine tool to another automatically as the operation is completed. The new setup accomplishes more than a conventional production line of more than fifteen machines and cuts a production run of several weeks down to a few days.

In estimating "how fast" and "how far" we must not lose sight of the fact that not all industries are susceptible to automation to the same extent. Some it will only touch, and some it will take over. It has been estimated that as little as 8 per cent of the labor force are in industries which will approach total automation and that perhaps 25 per cent are in industries where substantial automation is likely.

Automation will progress most rapidly in those industries where the whole procedure can be reduced to a continuous process, as in oil refining, flour milling, and chemicals. Other industries where production is now discrete may eventually be reorganized into a continuous flow, but only if the machinery to do it becomes economically justifiable.

In the mass production industries (like automobiles, radio, and television) automatic machinery is being introduced at different stages, but assembly is still largely a hand operation. The machinery exists to do it automatically in some cases, but is still too expensive to justify its use. For example, an automatic machine to solder circuit boards was developed but not used because it was found that the hand method was more economical. The progress of automation will be faster for fabricating than for assembling.

A second group of industries includes those in which extensive rather than full automation is probable. Examples are transportation, the production of nonstandardized consumer products, and large-scale retailing. In the last, for example, automation will be applied to the massive record keeping that such an operation entails, but it is not likely to replace the sales clerk. Point-of-sales recorders are currently being developed to do automatic charge account billing, inventory control, merchandise accounting, and to provide sales clerk and branch-store identification.

The industries which will be least affected by automation are those in which the element of personal service is very important, as in the professions; where the unit of operation is very small, as in most retailing; or where there are special conditions like space and weather as in agriculture. This does not mean that automation will not touch these fields. In medicine, for example, it could add greatly to diagnostic and surgical procedures. It is quite conceivable that a computer will be fed samples, readings, and other information which it would then analyze in order to compute the probable diagnosis.

What factors will determine how fast automation will come and how far it will go?

First, automation takes time. The reorganization of an office or factory is not accomplished overnight. A computer is not simply bought, plugged in, and put to work. Automation must be preceded by an extensive period of study if it is to be successful. Even after the installation is made a period of learning or "de-bugging" may be required. For example, it took the Great Lakes Pipe Line Company five and one-half years and $140,000 for research before it installed an automatic scheduling system. A large insurance company took two years to analyze its procedure before installing a computer. As industry acquires a backlog of experience and knowledge the progress of automation may be accelerated.

Second, the extension of automation will require specially trained personnel, engineers, people who can program the computers and set up the tapes, and maintenance men who can handle the extremely complex machinery. None of these is readily available to the company considering automation.

Third, management must be educated to use fully the equipment it buys. Sometimes an expensive computer is bought for a specific job which it accomplishes in a few hours a day. It then remains idle, an obvious waste of money, and discourages consideration of further purchases.

Fourth, existing manufacturing equipment that still

fulfills it function, although less automatically than possible, will act as a brake even in those industries where automation is most feasible. Our existing industrial plant is not being used to its fullest capacity. Even in our most prosperous years industry uses only about 80 per cent of its capacity.

We must conclude, therefore, that we are in no danger of being overwhelmed by "push-button" factories before we have a chance to plan adequately for the change. The attitude prevalent during the first industrial revolution when the displaced worker was thrown on his own inadequate resources is not possible in this era of social responsibility and strong unions. In 1950 Norbert Wiener, of the Massachusetts Institute of Technology, stated in his book *The Human Use of Human Beings* (published by Houghton Mifflin Company) that the new automatic machines were "the precise economic equivalent of slave labor" and could cause the worst depression in history. In 1956, however, he added:

> Since [then], I have participated in two big meetings with representatives of business management, and I have been delighted to see the awareness on the part of a great many of those present of the social dangers of our new technology and the social obligations of . . . management . . . to see that the new modalities are used for the benefit of man.

There is no doubt that we can adjust our economy to accomplish this aim and little doubt that we will. We cannot say with any assurance that a certain percentage of American production will be fully or half automated at a given time. Too much depends on technological developments, on military needs, and other broad economic factors. But by continued close study of the progress of automation as it occurs, we can develop a pattern of successful procedures to minimize individual hardships.

In a dynamic, growing economy automation will mean a new high standard of living and leisure and in Wiener's phrase, the "human use of human beings."

4 LEISURE

Leisure's Not for Loafing

Leisure as we know it today in the United States is a new phenomenon. Never before have so many people had so much free time and so much money with which to enjoy it. Traditionally the man who worked and produced had no spare time, and, conversely, the man who had leisure did not work productively. Members of the leisure class could indulge in politics, war, or religion. It was the mark of the aristocrat that he did not produce the necessities of life but only consumed them. Social status and free time belonged together to a small group.

The United States started out without a leisure class although eventually the rich got rich enough to be idle. America was a young, underdeveloped land, and it took long hours of hard labor to supply the basic needs of the community. Idleness was frowned upon, and the day of rest was justified by religious observance. Social philosophy supported economic need, and hard labor was looked upon as the good and true way of life.

Time off from work, and there was very little of it, was a period of rest and recuperation to prepare for the next day's work. This was just as true for the housewife as for the workingman. There were no prepared foods and electric appliances to relieve her, and no union to blow a five o'clock whistle for him. The sterner forms of Christian theology equated pleasure with immorality, and the adages that adorned the samplers taught that "Satan finds work for idle hands" and "idleness is wickedness."

But in the 1930's, in the years of the great depression, leisure—if we define it simply as free time—was suddenly thrust upon the American people in large quantities. Leisure became synonymous with idleness, and freedom from work became freedom to stagnate. This excess leisure was freedom in a dangerous form, and writers of the period predicted that technological unemployment would form a large class of permanently unemployed parasites who would only degenerate in their idleness.

How far we have come in twenty-five years toward adjusting our economy and our social outlook! Today we have tremendous productivity and consumption instead of the predicted idleness and degeneracy. Today we call leisure "the gift of the machine," and plan for its full and constructive use. Today's challenge to government and society is for all who have leisure time to be given also the opportunity to use it for greater development and self-fulfillment.

Perhaps the most socially important fact about the new leisure is that time away from work, rather than work itself, is coming to dominate the week. Work in this sense means the part of the week devoted to earning a living, or in the case of a woman, the part of the week devoted to essential housekeeping and/or earning a living. There is no intent of equating leisure (time away from work) with laziness or loafing. In that sense there is very little leisure in America. Every hammock in the back yard is flanked by the lawnmower and the rake. Leisure work is very often more strenuous than earning a living. For many sedentary workers leisure activities are the nearest they come to physical labor. For the purpose of this discussion, then, we will define leisure not simply as free time, but as time off from work that is filled with some unpaid activity undertaken either by choice for recreation or because of some need other than earning a living.

For the nine-to-five man the workweek is gradually being shortened with no loss of income and with added security in the form of guaranteed annual wages, social insurance, and spreading pension plans. He is the new addition to the leisure class. Social status and leisure have been separated. Today it is the very groups who are considered to be near the top of the occupational ladder, the self-employed professionals and the executives who take the office home in a briefcase, who have least time off.

Even among the college group from whom the professionals and business executives come, there is a marked decline in the kind of ambition for a career which can dominate a man's life. Note the results of the study made by David Riesman, sociologist at the University of Chicago.

An analysis of a series of interviews with the seniors of the class of 1955 was made in an attempt to determine what the students expected their life to be like in fifteen years. After allowing for the unreliability of much of the material, the conclusion was inescapable that the

driving ambition characterizing the economically insecure graduate of the 1930's has been replaced by a
vision of "life on a plateau"—a good job, large family,
and pensioned retirement. The graduate of 1955 felt
sure that a good job and security were his for the taking,
but he was neither interested in becoming president of
the company nor was he particularly interested in starting a small business of his own, and making it big.

His kind of ambition will not consume the time and
energy which his father used up in getting established
by trial and error. He will have more time and thought
for family living, friends, civic and religious participation, and all kinds of recreational activities. In fact, one
of the reasons why the interviews were turned over to
the Center for the Study of Leisure at the University of
Chicago was that so many of the students seemed concerned with hunting and fishing, golf, boating, and puttering.

Far from being considered wasteful and sinful, this
new leisure must be regarded as economically, as well as
personally, important. It is not only the fact that the
leisure is available, but even more the fact that leisure is
used actively; we play, we build, we travel, all with the
best possible equipment. Even when we sit in the back
yard or lounge on the beach it takes specially designed
furniture, sun shields, clothes, portable radios, and photographic equipment for, after all, we are exposed to the
neighbors as well as the sun.

Billions for Leisure

The steady increase in leisure has resulted in the
growth of many industries directly related to the public's
use of its free time. It has helped absorb the products

of our growing productive ability. Educational and cultural activities pursued during leisure hours will increase our reserve of human resources.

The study of the relation between increased leisure and the consumption of commodities is a fascinating and potentially profitable subject. The market for leisure expenditures is becoming one of the most active components of the American economy. The New York Stock Exchange points out that in ten years the market value of twenty-five companies catering to leisure time needs has risen sharply with top increases of 1,285 per cent for Hammond Organ, and 1,192 per cent for Outboard Marine.

The size of the market has been estimated between 30 billion and 40 billion dollars or approximately 15 per cent of total consumer expenditures. This amount is equivalent to what we spend for housing, and can even stand comparison with our enormous defense budget of 40 billion dollars. The main reason for the wide variation in estimates is the fact that some items can be included or excluded, depending on the writer's point of view. To what extent, for example, is tobacco a compulsion and to what extent is it used to add to relaxation in free time? What part of automobile expenses can properly be assigned to recreation?

During 1957 expenditures for strictly recreational activities, as classified by the Department of Commerce, reached 16 billion dollars, but this figure excluded some major leisure activities such as vacation travel and "do-it-yourself" projects. Recent estimates put vacation travel expenditures as high as 18 billion dollars, and even a conservative estimate would not be below 15 billion dollars annually. As for the wide range of "do-it-yourself" activities, they may not be recreation for many home owners, but they certainly take up a substantial part of his leisure time and involve the expenditure of a substantial amount of money.

Mechanization of industry created leisure for the workingman; automation will increase it. In the last century, productivity—that is production per man-hour —has been multiplied nearly six times. As a nation, we have taken this increased productivity in two forms, in an increased volume of goods and services and in an increase in leisure time. The long-term proportion has been about two-thirds of the increase in goods and services and one-third in leisure. The average workweek has declined from around 70 hours to nearly 40 hours, and pressure for cutting it further is strong.

Some important unions are preparing to make the shorter workweek their next big bargaining issue, and, despite the objections of individual industrialists that a shorter workweek will reduce the standard of living, there is little doubt that the decline will continue at least in the neighborhood of the historical average of three hours a decade. History has never justified the claim that a cut in the workweek would reduce the standard of living.

More Education for Many

An increase in free time can be taken in forms other than the direct reduction of hours, and the way in which we distribute free time will affect the pattern of spending for leisure activities.

For example, we may keep our children in school longer, thus reducing the number of years devoted to earning a living. The advance in this area has been encouraging during the last fifty years, but there is still plenty of room for improvement. A generation ago the typical adult had perhaps a year in high school; today about half graduate from high school and about 15 per cent go through two years of college. There are almost twice as many high school graduates in our adult population today as there were in 1940. In 1900 approximately 5 per cent of the population from 18 to 21 years of age were enrolled in school; by 1950 the figure had increased to 30 per cent.

The current pressure for more educational opportunity for all who can profit from it is only partially Sputnik-inspired. Industry and labor share the view that we must develop all our human resources if we are to retain our position of world leadership.

Executives are expected to be literate as well as hardheaded these days. Many are going back to school during work or leisure hours to study, not technology or business administration, but the humanities. The Bell Telephone Company, a leader in the back-to-school movement, sends its executives through a ten-month course at the Institute for Executives of the University of Pennsylvania. The International Ladies Garment Workers Union has long had classes for its members in all kinds of cultural activities not related to their work, and the United Steelworkers of America recently spent 2 million dollars to have its members study the humanities and arts at state universities.

The movement toward adult education, although not new, has broadened in the postwar years. The sponsors, in addition to corporations and unions, include local school systems and universities, and less formal groups such as those organized by the Ford Foundation for Adult Education and the Great Books Foundation. The kind of studying done is so varied that we could probably start with art and end with zoology, skipping but few letters in between.

The increase in the general level of schooling will affect adult recreation habits like the extent and type of reading, the extent and type of television viewing, and the popularity of the performing arts. It will increase the minority who listen to serious music, read more difficult books, and look for something beyond the red-barn-and-snow scene for their art.

The complex machinery which will characterize the era of automation may require fewer hands to run, but it will require more brains to design and maintain. Education—in technology to deal with the machines and in the social sciences to deal with the human problems of the nation and the world—is one form of leisure activity which must continue its expansion.

Consumer expenditures for private education and research reached 3 billion dollars in 1957, of which 1.2 billion dollars was for higher education. This is just about one-fifth of what we spent in the same year for tobacco products. However, higher education cannot be fully supported by the student body; to the extent that we admit students according to their ability to pay rather than their ability to learn we neglect to develop part of our human resources. Education at all levels will need more support, both public and private.

Time to Retire

At the far end of the age scale, the increase in available free time has been brought about largely by the advancing life expectancy. In 1900 a person could expect to live to an average of 49 years; today's life expectancy is 70 years. The proportion of older people in the population is rising steadily. In 1955 there were 14 million people in this country 65 years or older; by 1975 the total is expected to increase to nearly 21 million. The present average retirement age is around 65 years —voluntary or forced by company policy. By 1975, if the retirement age declines to 60, we shall have 30 million people, in a sense, unemployed.

What are they to do with their time? What would they like to do and what can they afford to do?

It is unthinkable that a nation which privately and publicly has assumed so much responsibility for the welfare of its citizens should say that after 60 or 65 years of age a man or woman who has worked for a good part of his life must now be content with a subsistence level of existence. That is the status of much of our older population today. Even recent surveys have shown that the income level for the oldest part of our population is very low and leaves little for recreation after necessities have been supplied. This is still true despite remarkable progress in pension plans and retirement benefits, both public and private. The federal social security system alone pays over 5 billion dollars a year in pensions.

If the financial means for rewarding occupation cannot be supplied directly to the older part of the population, perhaps recreational facilities can be made available on a free or low-cost basis. Further study will be required to determine how best to fill this vacuum, but first the right of the elderly to constructive occupation must be recognized as basic.

In 1956 a legal start was made toward supplying the special housing needs of the aged, and with it some thought was given to recreational problems. Among other provisions of the law is a clause providing financial assistance to qualified sponsors for the purpose of de-

veloping apartment projects with living, dining, and
community recreational facilities particularly directed
toward the comfort of the aged. It is also now generally
recognized that "retirement colonies" should afford
easily accessible churches, libraries, and theatres.

Mass Market for Leisure

In between the student and retired worker is the 20 to
64 year age group, from which the bulk of the labor
force is drawn. These are the people with time and
money, and it is their needs, habits, and tastes which
will determine the main growth patterns of the leisure
market.

Increased industrial productivity has been absorbed
through a higher standard of living and an increase in
time off from work. In recent years there has been a
tendency to shorten the working period through paid
vacations and holidays, in addition to cuts in the workweek.

Studies by the National Industrial Conference Board
have shown that 99 per cent of the companies surveyed
give paid vacations to hourly employees, compared with
only 46 per cent before the Second World War; that 96
per cent give paid holidays compared with only 14 per
cent before the war; and, that only about 18 per cent
have a two-week ceiling on vacations for hourly employees, compared with 80 per cent who maintained the
two-week ceiling only ten years ago.

In analyzing the leisure market, a cut in the workweek
and an increase in paid vacations cannot be lumped together simply as more time off. When a man gets a few
hours extra a week, he is likely to read a little more,
watch a little more television, perhaps putter around the

workshop a little more. If he can arrange his hours so
that he works four days instead of five, and if the third
day off is Friday or Monday, he is likely to pack the
family in the car for a short trip much more frequently
than he did when the week-end was only two days. If,
on the other hand, the workweek does not change much
but a week of paid vacation is added, he will almost
surely pack the family in the car and go—to family,
friends, motels, or hotels—but go he most certainly will.

So vacation-minded are we becoming, that the National Association of Travel Organizations is conducting
a campaign—and getting support—to change the observance of certain major holidays to Mondays, to make
five long week-ends a year. Thus we would celebrate
President's Day on the third Monday in February, Memorial Day on the fourth Monday in May, Independence Day on the first Monday in July, and Thanksgiving
Day on the fourth Monday in November.

The four-day week is currently emerging as a major
labor issue and will be pressed for strongly, as automation spreads. The UAW is definitely pointing to a 32-hour week of four days as a nearby goal. Paid vacations
will also become more widespread and longer. Although
perhaps not a major bargaining issue, they will be included as fringe benefits.

How much money is available for spending during
this leisure time? The answer is simple—"Plenty, and
more to come." Disposable personal income, that is, the
amount the consumer has left after taxes, started climbing in 1938 and has continued uninterrupted ever since.
In 1946 disposable income was 161 billion dollars; by
1957 it had reached 305 billion dollars. By 1960 it will
probably increase to 500 billion dollars. Of course the
rising cost of living took its share during the postwar

period, but much of the gain in income is reflected in
increased purchases of goods and services. Discretionary spending power (the amount left over after taxes
and necessities are paid for) represented one-third of
consumer income in 1940; today it represents nearly 60
per cent. In 1946, 33 per cent of American families had
incomes over $4,000; by 1956 the proportion had risen
to over 60 per cent.

Part of the increase in family income is earned by
working wives, and there are more and more each year.
In 1940 there were some 14 million women in the labor
force and 36 per cent were married. In 1955 there were
20 million women in the labor force and 59 per cent
were married. This increase occurred despite the emphasis on family living, houses instead of apartments to
be taken care of, and more babies. Although working
women subtract from the total leisure time available to
the population, they add materially to the money the
family can spend in the time it has together. Home sew-
ing, casual reading, fancy cooking, and club meetings
may suffer, but the big beneficiaries include the vacation
and entertainment industries, restaurants, and food processing.

An analysis of the big leisure market shows three
major trends. First is the switch from spectator and
group to active individual sports and, in general, the
growing relative importance of all forms of active recreation. Second is the filtering down from upper to lower
income brackets of recreational activities which were
once in the luxury class. Third is the influence of suburban living and the emphasis on family activities.

Back in 1934 the National Recreation Association
made a survey to find out what people did with their

leisure time, and what they would like to do. The results
showed the first ten leisure occupations were:

1. Reading newspapers and magazines.
2. Radio.
3. Movies.
4. Visiting and entertaining.
5. Books (fiction).
6. Automobile riding.
7. Swimming.
8. Writing letters.
9. Books (nonfiction).
10. Conversation.

while the preference was for:

1. Tennis.
2. Swimming.
3. Boating.
4. Golf.
5. Camping.
6. Gardening.
7. Playing a musical instrument.
8. Automobile riding.
9. Theatre.
10. Ice skating.

Without taking the results of the survey too literally,
we can use it to illustrate two of the major trends in leisure enjoyment. Highest on the list of actual activities,
and dominating it, were inactive occupations—reading,
movies, radio. Dominating the preferred list were active
sports—tennis, swimming, boating, golf.

A switch to the active use of leisure in the United

States is not surprising. We are not a contemplative society; we have always prided ourselves on concrete accomplishments. Loafing was never considered quite respectable, and even today when we have time to spare we generally feel that we must go somewhere, make something, catch up our reading, or the time is wasted.

With hours of work declining and much of the hardest physical labor being taken over by the machine, even the active production worker has enough physical energy left after work to do more than recuperate in preparation for the next day's labor. The growing army of office and other sedentary workers need some active change during leisure hours.

Indirectly, television has been partly responsible for the increase in active leisure pastimes. Being easily available and free (in the sense that it could be turned on without paying), it supplies much of the need for passive recreation and frequently leaves the viewer with the feeling that he has sat long enough. It has absorbed part of the time and money formerly devoted to movies and to spectator sports since it supplies entertainment of much the same caliber as the movies, and televises many of the sports events which formerly took time and money to get to. It also has absorbed part of the additional leisure time as it has become available.

Movie admissions have remained almost static since 1952—having declined from a pretelevision peak in 1946. Admissions to spectator sports have also remained practically static in the last ten years, and spectator events frequently cannot get an audience. On the other hand, admissions to commercial participant amusements have increased 42 per cent since 1952; sales of wheel goods, durable toys, sports equipment, boats and pleasure aircraft have jumped 52 per cent in the same period. These were the two largest increases in the recreation category, aside from television and radio repair, which is certainly a recreation expense but hardly a participant form of entertainment.

The switch to individual active sports has been a boon to the industries supplying them. Previously there were two kinds of sports stores, the specialists in team equipment for clubs and schools and those which supplied the luxury market for golf, hunting, and fishing. Today the bulk of the business is in medium and low-priced sports equipment for individual use, although the team and luxury markets still exist.

Hunting and fishing are good examples of the growing market for individual sports equipment. In 1933, 5 million fishing licenses were issued in the United States. Twenty years later the total had more than tripled. In the same period the number of hunting licenses issued increased from 6 million to 15 million.

Probably the most important beneficiary of the "let's go" urge is the group of small and large industries that cater to vacationing Americans—the hotels, motels, gas stations, diners, automobile maintenance shops. We can only estimate the amount of money spent for vacation travel since there are no consistent reports which break travel components down into pleasure and business use. Total recreational travel, domestic and foreign, including the money spent staying at hotels, must reach 15 billion dollars annually.

Most of the traveling is done by car. All the data pertaining to car use show increases during the last five years. Purchases of new and used cars were up 38 per cent; sales of tires, tubes, accessories, and parts were up

21 per cent; automobile care, repair, parking, storage, and rental 36 per cent; sales of gasoline and oil 55 per cent; bridge, tunnel, ferry, and road tolls up 67 per cent. The amount spent on airline travel doubled during the same period. Intercity railway and bus lines have been unable to compete successfully, and both showed declining revenues during this period of expanding travel.

Of course, not all the increase in car use is for vacations; families moving to the suburbs find the car a necessity for daily living, but having once bought it they are likely to use it for recreation and during their vacations. Passenger car registration has doubled since 1940. Approximately 70 million people take automobile vacations each year; 85 per cent of vacation travel is done by car.

All the industries which feed, house, and supply equipment for "America on wheels" have further expansion to look forward to. Public expenditures, mainly in the form of new and better roads and further development of national and state parks, will encourage the expansion.

Wherever public facilities have been developed they have attracted large numbers of tourists. Almost half the states consider travel a leading industry. Tennessee, Kentucky, and Alabama have found that the artificial lakes built by the Tennessee Valley Authority have supplied excellent boating and fishing to large numbers of visitors. State and national parks receive over 200 million visitors each year. They offer a wide variety of activities—hiking, sight-seeing, camping, swimming, boating, and fishing—at low costs, which makes them attractive to families without too much to spend.

Homogenized Leisure

Tastes in leisure activities filter down from the "upper classes" and work their way up from the lower occupational levels. Rolf B. Meyerson of the Center for the Study of Leisure at the University of Chicago illustrated this two-way traffic by pointing out that as golf is no longer exclusively an upper class game playing pool is not confined to the lower social groups. Leisure activities differ little from one neighborhood to the next, despite variation in occupational and social levels.

I might add, to the extent that income permits, and with some change in form where income differences make it necessary. Two income groups may go in for boating, but one man's yacht becomes another man's rowboat with outboard motor, and deep sea fishing in foreign waters becomes bait casting in a nearby lake. For American industry numerous outboard motors and 18 million fishermen are more profitable than a few yachts and a few stuffed and mounted sail fish.

For a really booming industry nothing beats boating, today one of America's leading family sports. In 1957, 30 million people spent 1.5 billion dollars on boating. This includes purchases of new and used boats, accessories, safety equipment, fuel, insurance, docking, and maintenance. In 1947 there were 2.4 million recreational boats in use in the United States; just ten years later, by 1957, there were 6.5 million on all waters of the United States, one for every 28 persons in the country. Small craft with outboard motors are the bulk of the 6.5 million, with sailboats a distant second.

Outboard boating has outgrown the fisherman and is now used by the whole family for cruising, water skiing, and picknicking as well as for fishing. As a result, there has been a trend toward larger boats and heavier motors. In 1941 motors sold averaged 3.6 horsepower; in 1956 they averaged 14.2 horsepower. The boating industry is quick to point out that "our lakes, streams, and salt water bays offer practically the last uncrowded scenes for outdoor activity." At the rate we are going, this may not be true very much longer.

It is definitely the new leisure class and not the traditional one which is expanding the boating business. In 1956, 65 per cent of the boats and 63 per cent of the motors were bought by skilled and semiskilled workers, and clerical and sales personnel. The largest single category was skilled workers, who bought 39 per cent of the motors and 37 per cent of the boats.

Sociologists have been trying to determine what influences taste—whether people who find themselves with more time on their hands look to see what their neighbors do with their leisure, or whether they look to the occupations higher in the prestige scale for their cues. Veblen points out in his classic *Theory of the Leisure Class* that certain occupations, like hunting and fishing, honored originally in barbaric society, became associated with the leisure class as it developed. Although the original reasons for honoring these occupations have long disappeared, the very fact that they remained the sole prerogative of the traditional leisure class gave them a definite prestige value.

What is more natural than that the American who wants to advance to a higher financial and professional status should also wish to become "upper class" in his spare time? What more natural than that he should try to confirm his new status as a member of the honored leisure class by adopting the pleasures formerly reserved to it?

The Home as a Leisure Center

In money spent, out-of-home activities far exceed the at-home leisure occupations, but in time spent, the second group is much more important. Approximately 70 per cent of all leisure time is spent at home. The reason? Social scientists have given many—that people choose to stay at home as an escape from the complex world of problems, judgments, and opinions; that in and around the house there are opportunities for expressing the urge of craftsmanship which is generally lacking in today's mechanized work. The most obvious reason has been somewhat neglected. In-home activities like reading and television cost less, or, like basic gardening and home repair, they must be done. In addition, they require no baby sitters.

As far as occupying time at home, television has no close rival. Regardless of occupational level, television is listed first as a leisure occupation, and the average family is reported to run its set more than 6 hours a day. Radio comes second. After that leisure occupations vary somewhat, according to occupational levels. More than 3.5 billion dollars were spent on radio and television sales and repair, records, and musical instruments in 1957. Reading in all forms, books, magazines, and newspapers, took approximately 3 billion dollars.

Probably the most important home activity as far as expenditures go is "do-it-yourself," that all-inclusive term which can cover anything from home permanents to home repair—the whole gamut of activities in which the layman performs a function previously performed by a professional. The volume of the composite "do-it-yourself" industry for home improvement and repair (without the home permanents) has been estimated at around 6 billion dollars annually, and if this figure seems high it must be remembered that today's homeowners paint, wallpaper, landscape, add rooms, finish attics and basements, lay terraces, and keep the plumbing in repair. Advice to the handy man can be found in newspaper columns, magazine articles, and complete magazines and books devoted to his interests. A 1954 survey of the Department of Commerce showed that homeowners had purchased 1.5 billion dollars worth of materials for home improvement in five months, and most of this material was put in place by the homeowners themselves.

Just how much of this work is done for recreation is practically impossible to determine. Many a homeowner would be loath to admit that the lawn he loved five years ago has become at best just a chore to be done. He might just as well admit to his neighbor that he can't afford to hire a gardener or that he is getting too old to like work.

The origin of "do-it-yourself" is in the move to the suburbs. In the period since 1950, during which the total United States civilian population increased 9 per cent, suburban parts of metropolitan markets grew 34 per cent. Not all this movement was by choice; in large part it was due to the housing shortage which followed the Second World War.

Faced with substandard living conditions, or the prospect of living with relatives, and encouraged by the liberal terms of the G.I. mortgage, many young families that could not otherwise have afforded it, bought their own homes. It was then up to them to maintain the property in good condition and see that at least it looked no worse than the others on the block. And they generally managed that and more. Mother took an adult

education course in gardening, and father bought some
tools and started to read "how-to" books. If he was a
veteran he probably got a head start by learning some
mechanical skill in the Armed Forces.

For many people there is a good deal of enjoyment in
the doing and pride in the accomplishment. Work in
and around the home can satisfy a long-neglected need
to make something of permanent value or something of
beauty. The work doesn't have to be perfect (and seldom is), but if the basement, instead of being waste
space, now has walls, a floor, and a ceiling the homeowner will be proud to say, "I did it myself." Work in
the garden or around the house can also be a welcome
change of pace from housekeeping or the office, and may
relieve some of the tensions engendered by both.

Growing families and unused space are a combination
that the handy man finds hard to resist, and if he can
manage to resist, his wife usually can't. So the local
stores sell more lumber, nails, paint, floor covering, and
power tools.

Accurate statistics on the individual industries that
compose the "do-it-yourself" market have not been com-
piled, but sales of home workshop tools are estimated to
have quadrupled since the boom started. Approximately
75 to 80 per cent of home painting is done by the homeowner. Retail lumber yard sales have profited more
than many other outlets since many a handy man who
wouldn't dare to touch the plumbing or the electricity
feels there is no risk except to his thumb in cutting and
hammering wood.

The industries which supply the "do-it-yourself" markets have helped themselves by helping the handy man.
They have concentrated on developing easy-to-use tools,
paints, and painting equipment. They have changed the

standard size of available wood panels to make it easier for the layman to use. They have put out kits and plans, many of the latter being free for the asking.

"Do-it-yourself" has been called both a fad and a hobby. It is neither, although it contains an element of both. Mostly it is part of homeowning, and it will remain an important leisure activity.

Games, crafts, and hobbies are taking up more time than they used to. Volume in adult games has risen about 150 per cent in the last ten years, while sales of crafts and hobby materials increased from about 3 million dollars to 300 million dollars in the same period. In neither case could any substantial part of the increase be written off as a rise in prices.

In the hobby market the increase was due largely to the introduction of three new products: painting by numbers, plastic kits, and ready-to-run HO electric trains. The first, generally an adult activity, is clearly a quick way of producing something which one can say he made himself, without the need to develop any real skill or imagination. All cater to a desire to get something done without doing much.

Leisure—A Look at the Future

Studying the leisure market is a problem for industry and sociologists; thus far the sociologists have been ahead. The leisure market is rich and developing, and the businessman that keeps one step ahead of it will more fully realize its potential. If houses are built, lawn mowers will be needed. If the home and garden magazines feature "how to build your own terrace," someone can start promoting outdoor lighting for leisure hours after dark.

Not the least important of the new industries which will grow with the new leisure is the research by social scientists for industry to determine which activities will become more important and which will decline; to probe the depths of whatever subconscious we may have, to decide if we buy a boat because boating is relaxing for the whole family, or we see in it the "snob appeal" of a yacht, or a return to childhood's toy sailboat; whether leisure activities should be promoted as family fun or as pleasure (a word which still has some connotations of sin); whether we have sufficiently outgrown our Puritan ancestry and can just enjoy ourselves, or whether it is better to give the advertisements a more pragmatic slant.

Perhaps the most significant feature of tomorrow's leisure activities is that they will be even more centered around family living as the suburbs and the families in them keep growing. The basic importance of the family as a center of activity was succinctly summarized by Margaret Mead: "As once it was wrong to play so hard that it might affect one's work, now it is wrong to work so hard that it may affect family life."

The emphasis on the family will mean the continued importance of "do-it-yourself," gardening, family games and hobbies, travel-by-car with the children, picknicking, camping, boating. Less commercially important, but very time consuming, will be the numerous community and religious participations—the Parent-Teacher Associations, the Little Leagues, the Scouts, the school board meetings, the voters' organizations, and the community arts councils.

The importance of the home and the amount of time spent in and around it will increase the mixing of the husband and wife roles. Nowadays father brings home the money for the bacon and then goes to the supermarket to bring home the bacon itself. The next step is cooking, and not only on the background barbecue. One New York department store already reports more male interest in cooking with resulting sales of spices, herbs, and fancy equipment. On the other hand, as the woman goes along on the boat or fishing trip we shall have "new looks" in fishing rods and hip boots.

We can also expect some maturing in public taste as different forms of leisure activity are tried and fail to produce much besides boredom. Adult education through school programs and less formal study groups will become, in itself, not only a more popular leisure activity but will also help direct other activities into more constructive channels. We can hope for more educational programs on television after the success of the "Sunrise Semester," and we can expect the success of the better paperbacks to continue as people get time to absorb as well as to read books.

The question of leisure cannot be confined to how much money there will be and how it will be spent. The larger problem is whether we will feel satisfied after we have spent our time and money. Do we take part in civic activities because we consider them worthwhile or because of social pressure? Do we need education for leisure as part of education for living? Shall we use at least part of our leisure for some constructive purpose or are we really entitled to play and loaf no matter how much free time we have?

There is a developing thought among social scientists that people should be taught how to use their spare time better, so that leisure may be used creatively rather than being dissipated. One exponent of this viewpoint is Willard C. Sutherland, Director of Personnel Services of the National Recreation Association. He wrote, "Since the average citizen is unable to invent new uses for his leisure, a professional elite shares a heavy responsibility for discovering criteria for ways of employing leisure and creating enthusiasms for common ends within the moral aims of the community." This quotation makes leisure sound more like work than play. It can be attacked on the ground that too much organizing and directing will spoil all the fun, but, considering the amount of time involved, we can at least introduce "the average citizen" to different leisure activities.

There is an old story which goes back to the days when the early unions won their first concession in shorter hours for the garment workers in New York City. Having nothing better to do, one man put on his best suit and took his best girl for a walk. Paying more attention to the girl than to where he was walking, he brushed against some wet paint and got the good suit all smeared. "Damn the Union!" he exclaimed, "If I were working instead of walking I wouldn't get into trouble."

Do we know better how to use our free time now? Alfred C. Clarke, in a survey on the use of leisure, suggests that few people get the satisfaction they want from their use of leisure. The professional group is the most discontented. An illustration is the kind of comment that was added to the question about how much time was spent on television. Examples were "More than I should," "Don't enjoy many of the programs but there's nothing else to do," and, "Guess it's just a habit."

Concern with our use of leisure is not just awakening, although certainly it is getting more of the attention it deserves. Almost twenty-five years ago William Butterworth, formerly president of the United States Chamber of Commerce, wrote that it should be of general concern that the new spare time be used advantageously and that it should not be a cause for deterioration of workmanship or citizenship.

I do not mean to imply that recreation is in any way wasteful. On the contrary, satisfying recreation is essential to individual and community health. But when a leisure activity is undertaken simply because there is nothing else to do or because every one else is doing it, then we had better take time to consider just where the new emphasis on leisure is taking us. If we can regard free time as a raw material, we will come to think more in terms of its constructive use.

5 | CULTURE

Symphonies and Soap Operas

Culture in America is big business. It is a 10 billion dollar industry comparable in size to today's electronics industry or to the amount spent by all the states in the nation to perform their multitude of services for the common welfare. This fact cannot be overlooked when making an appraisal of its values, its impact, and its future development. As in other big industries, the producers of culture must sell their products and, therefore, to a large extent will produce what is most salable. But since the cultural products of a society are so often used as a measure of its worth and maturity, this industry and society with it must also foster those forms of culture which have a more restricted appeal and which cannot pay for themselves.

The term "culture" has been used for many different concepts. In its broadest sociological meaning, it includes the habits, arts, and institutions which differentiate one society from another. In its narrowest connotation, it includes only the fine arts, understood and appreciated only by a trained and intelligent elite. Folk art may sometimes be included in this narrow definition if its origins are far enough away in space or time to make it respectable.

For our purposes, culture is neither as broad as the sociologists indicate nor so narrow as to encompass only the serious artist. It includes, in addition to the latter, the phenomenon which has been called "Mass Culture" or the "Public Arts." Although both phases are important, and both have economic facets which should be explored, they must be treated separately. For the most part they are produced by different methods, performed by different artists, and sold to different audiences.

There is an area of overlapping and occasional differences of opinion as to which side of the railroad tracks a particular work comes from, but for most of our cultural output there is no question. The Philharmonic is at one end of the yardstick, and the latest crooner at the other, with the center of gravity way down near the crooner.

Development of Culture in America

America has long been accused of being a strictly materialistic society, interested only in new gadgets and bigger cars with no time, inclination, or the intellectual capacity for serious art or literature. Europe has always boasted of its painters, its writers, and its performing artists. The United States prides itself on its industrial know-how and high standard of living. These opposing values are part of a completely different historical development.

At the time when the United States was emerging as a nation, culture in Europe was the province of the aristocracy, the small group with inherited wealth, leisure,

and the privilege of education. There was no comparable class in the United States. Here the people wanted
better homes, better education, generally better living
conditions, and they were willing to work long and hard
to get them. The rivers had to be bridged, the moun-
tains mined, and the railroads built, and whatever time
they had left was devoted to hammering out the political
and economic form the new country would take. The
arts were left to the women, not exactly a leisure class
either, and thus they came to be considered "sissy stuff."

The serious artists who did appear were alienated
from their own society. They looked for their audiences
in Europe and were generally contemptuous of Americans. When a leisure class emerged in the United
States, financially able to support the arts, they also
looked to Europe; the European artist had a prestige
which the American, trained in America, did not have.

Artistically, America was a colony of Europe. The
aspiring American singer had to go to Europe for training and experience and frequently had to adopt a foreign
name and a fake foreign accent before being accepted
by a respected opera company. An American performer
or an American work of art was on the defensive simply
because it was American.

But America is growing up. A high standard of living
has been achieved, and science and brain power rather
than long hours of physical labor will help us maintain
and expand it. We have the capacity to create and the
leisure to appreciate the fine arts. We now export as well
as import artistic achievements. Many American authors—Hemingway, Faulkner, Steinbeck—are read not
only in Europe but also in South America, Japan, and
the Soviet Union. American paintings are exhibited in
the art centers of France, England, and Italy. Part of

the first Ford Foundation grant to the creative arts will go toward sponsoring American operas.

The fine arts are not now, or are they likely to become, big business. However, since they reflect an essential part of the spirit of our society, they have a place in the education and development of each one of us, not only as individuals but also in our economic capacity as worker, professional or businessman. No matter how many machines we employ as automation progresses, in the forseeable future we shall still be dealing with people and we must use all possible roads to reach a fuller understanding of our own society.

There are many signs of an awakening interest in the traditional forms of culture, popularly ridiculed as "longhair" or "egghead." Impressive as these are, in quantitative importance, the fine arts cannot begin to compete with the other form of culture which has mushroomed over the face of America. I refer, of course, to "mass culture."

It is not my purpose here to attempt a final appraisal of the material so widely circulated by television, radio, newspapers, and the other mass media. Sociologists, psychologists, and criminologists will long argue the extent to which the comics create juvenile delinquency; whether subconscious comparison between husbands and movie heroes raises the divorce rate, and whether our promising young artists are lured by gold away from serious artistic effort. Certainly, much of the printed material will find no one to defend it on its own merits, not the publishers who profit from it or the purchasers who hide it from the children. Good, bad, or just harmless, the size and scope of the industries involved must be understood in order to evaluate the economic importance of mass communications.

The industrial revolution provided the yeast for the rise of mass culture. It started with the earliest inventions in technology which made it possible and profitable to produce books, periodicals, and pictures cheap enough for mass circulation. Political democracy and popular education broke down the barrier which had for so long kept practically all culture a monopoly of the wealthy and aristocratic. Further industrialization relieved man of part of his manual labor and left him with unoccupied time, thus providing a market for the new form of culture it could now produce.

It is within our own time, however, that all the factors encouraging the growth of mass culture have become so pronounced that now it dominates the cultural structure of the country. Advancing mechanization has provided the leisure and thus the market. Radio, television, and improved printing methods have provided the means of distribution.

Basically, the "popular arts" differ from the "elite arts" in three respects. First, the final product in popular art is usually the result of teamwork, of groups hired to do specific jobs, unlike a poem or piece of sculpture which is the product of one man's creativity. Second, popular art is produced not because the artist must say something vital or even to please a patron or small group, but rather to satisfy the requirements of a large mass of people. This fact must determine the form it takes; certainly it must strictly limit the new and unusual. Last, rather than being performed for or circulated among a small group, popular art is distributed in overwhelming quantities by mechanical means. Because of this, the terms mass culture and mass media are frequently used interchangeably, although elite culture is sometimes distributed by mass media.

In what sense, then, can the popular arts be called arts in the accepted meaning of the word? For a very large majority of the people they serve one function that was served by the fine arts and folk arts. They provide diversion after the day's work (frequently highly monotonous in this age of mechanization) and satisfy, vicariously, the needs which cannot be fulfilled in ordinary lives. At least for the time the television is on, the children, the boss, and the bank account are out of mind as well as out of sight.

Americans Do Read

The mass media are well named; their audience is massive. Circulation of daily newspapers has been increasing steadily until current circulation of all dailies, excluding Sundays, is 57 million copies, approximately 12 newspapers for every 11 families in the United States.

Newspaper reading cannot be considered just a means of keeping up with the news. It is a kind of diversion in the same way that movies and magazines are. The column, comics, and commentaries are a good part of the reading material of many purchasers and help mold their opinions. The detailed accounts of murder and rape are set forth to provide excitement, not to give the status of crime in the United States.

The Sunday papers, even more than the dailies, are purchased for reading material rather than news. This is indicated most graphically by the rapid growth of the Sunday magazine sections, which increased their circulation by about 30 million in 10 years.

The increase in magazine circulation has been steady but less spectacular than the gain for magazine sections

in the last ten years. However, magazine circulation
grew rapidly between the two world wars. Prior to the
First World War there were 50 general and farm magazines per issue circulated for each 100 adults. By the
end of the Second World War the figure was 125; in
1955 it was 155.

Unhappily, we must include the comics in any study
of what circulates as reading material and how much
money is involved in mass culture. They cannot be dis-
missed as "kid stuff" and not part of adult reading. During the war, sales of comics at Post Exchanges far
outstripped sales of *Life, Reader's Digest,* and *The Saturday Evening Post* combined. None of these magazines
can be placed in the category of "elite culture," nor can
they be considered unsuitable for reading during a
period of extreme tension where escape would be a
prime motive in entertainment. One estimate places
sales of comics at ten times the sales of the three magazines, and to this figure must be added the borrowing
and exchanging which is popular among comic book
readers.

The economic weight of the comic book industry has
been summarized well by Gilbert Seldes in *The Great
Audience* (published by Viking Press, Inc.):

> The economic situation is a simple one. The newsstand
> receipts for comic books total seventy-two million dollars a
> year; the wholesale distributors of these books count on
> them for a third of their total magazine sales: . . . The
> field is dominated by a half dozen houses, each of which
> publishes a wide range of books; Western, romance, "scien-
> tific," murder and so on. Like the movies, they have de-
> veloped a system of block-booking which prevents the
> retailer from exercising any discretion: if he wants the best
> seller, he must take the others as well; he cannot eliminate
> those which bring disrepute.

Thus far the protests of Parent-Teacher Associations, church, and other civic groups have had little success in counterbalancing the weight of the 72 million dollars a year.

The book industry is the most interesting of the printed mass media from the economic viewpoint, because of the revolutions that have occurred within it, and the controversy over whether the "elite" part is being homogenized and degraded by economic pressures.

The book-publishing industry has been enjoying some prosperous years. This may seem surprising in view of published statements that the industry is facing a financial crisis, that it is impossible to publish an adult quality trade book profitably, that costs have risen fantastically. Actually, there is no real contradiction. It depends largely on whether we speak of the industry as a whole or try to separate new books, adult books, hardbound books.

Adult trade books are frequently published at a loss, but this loss is more than overbalanced by subsidiary income, that is, book club sales, movie rights, reprints, and serial publications. In fact, much of the alarm about the book business stems from this circumstance. Obviously if there is an economic need to offset a loss by sales to book clubs or motion picture producers, there is also an overwhelming inducement to take for publication the books which are most likely to be accepted.

In the last twenty-five years the circulation of books through book clubs has risen from 2 million to 50 million copies. The type of books they sell varies from those which concentrate on nonfiction—for example, science or history—to those which take as their criterion for selection content which can be passed on to the children without deletions. The mass market is somewhere in between.

To some extent the book club selections have replaced the handsomely bound, unread sets of classics which were once a required part of interior decorating. In many homes the new books serve the same function, presenting their best-seller titles for public inspection and turning their uncut pages to the wall.

The most common complaint among book publishers is that costs of production have risen far past the point where book prices can cover them. Whereas formerly a novel could break even at 3,000 copies, it now takes 7,500. Cheaper methods of production have been used where possible—cheaper bindings, paper instead of cloth, less illustration—but the only way out is volume circulation and subsidiary sales. So we are back to book clubs, movies, and reprints.

The Paperback Revolution

Inexpensive editions of established books are not entirely new; they were popular periodically between 1825 and 1900. Today's paperback revolution started in 1939 when Pocket Books put out their 25-cent reprints. Since that time, the use of advanced technical processes and the employment of the mass distribution machinery already established for magazines and newspapers have enabled the industry to satisfy a skyrocketing consumer demand. Volume in 1957 reached approximately 270 million copies, which sold for nearly 100 million dollars. By 1958 there were 6,000 titles in print, and circulation of some of the early issues had individually reached into the millions.

The all-time best seller, so far, in paperbacks is

Dr. Spock's *Baby and Child Care*, which has run up a total of nearly 10 million copies in the twelve years since its publication. Other paperback best sellers are Erskine Caldwell's *God's Little Acre*, which sold 7 million copies in the paper edition compared with 7,000 in a hard cover edition; *From Here to Eternity*, more than 3.5 million copies; Shakespeare's *Great Tragedies*, over 2 million; the *Illiad* and the *Odyssey*, one million each; and 30 million copies of seven Mickey Spillane titles.

This best seller list illustrates the wide and varied appeal of the paperbacks and demonstrates the growth in the industry since the days when a paper cover automatically meant junk to many readers. There has been a quality revolution within this revolution; a ready market has been discovered for all kinds of nonfiction—classics, science, plays, anthologies, the Bible, art reproductions, and how-to (raise your child, improve your personality, build your house, acquire peace of mind, identify genuine antiques, live with your ulcers) books. Since 1952 the biggest increase in the number of titles issued has been for nonfiction even in books selling as high as 75 cents, the category which includes novels, mysteries, and Westerns.

Of the 6,000 paperback titles available, approximately half are the higher-priced volumes which are priced between 75 cents and $1.95. They are designed to appeal to the educated public, students, and teachers, a market which is rapidly expanding. They offer scholarly books, science for the layman, and the classics of fiction and nonfiction at prices which even college professors can afford. They are being used in schools for supplementary reading and textbooks, and they are being added rapidly to college bookstores. New lines of higher-priced paperbacks are being added, and six university presses publish their own reprint series.

However, not even the widespread circulation of the higher-priced paperbacks has been accepted without criticism. Again economic necessity is accused of dictating the titles. The argument runs thus: Since initial printing for a mass market (low-priced) paperback runs around 100,000 and for a high-priced paperback, 20,000, the publisher must be assured of a large waiting market before he adds a title to his list. The list is therefore likely to include the classics but exclude the new young authors who might, if given a chance, become classics. In other words, what comparatively unknown name can compete against Shakespeare and Dante for the attention of the educated public?

This argument is less true today than it was a few years back. The list of titles being published is growing more varied, and new writers are being introduced, especially in collections. Paperbacks are no longer only reprints. Approximately 30 per cent of paperbacks today are new titles. In any case, the economic argument is incomplete. If the publication of paperback classics is profitable enough to nullify some of the loss entailed in the publication of new trade books, it is a help to the publisher who wants to introduce a new writer through the more usual channels of a hardbound book. Never in history has a new author been assured the circulation which a paperbound edition gives.

New Opium of the People

Wherever there is a critical opinion on America's cultural level, there will television and radio be, condemned for the massive transmission of trivia, for the production and preservation of the mass mind, for exploiting the lowest in public taste, in order to sell useless gadgets. Less often will there be a recognition of their function in mass distribution of some excellent programs. Fifty million people tuned in to see *Richard III;* 120,000 students turned on their television sets at 6:30 in the morning to the "Sunrise Semester," a college-level literature course given by New York University and then started a run on the bookstores for the books discussed; 12 million listeners tuned their radios in to a production of the new Barber-Menotti opera "Vanessa."

To the obvious answer that the number of such programs is infinitesimal compared with the mass of mediocrity, I must answer that, as every statistician and economist knows, a figure can look big or small, depending on what you compare it with. I think the comparison should be made with the number of people who would have heard or seen the work if it had not been broadcast. How many of the 50 million would have read even part of *Richard III?* How long would it take for the Metropolitan Opera House to reach an audience of 12 million, with its seating capacity of 3,616? Above all, how many will try a program of this type when it involves only the turn of a dial, but would not try it if it meant the price of a ticket and a trip downtown?

Wholesale condemnation of radio and television, without some appreciation of the best programs, will only discourage further attempts. Neither the media nor any group of critics, no matter how valid its point of view, can summarily change or channel public taste. Their object should be to encourage the best possible programs so that our most powerful means of communication are not confined to mediocrity and banality. Many members of the despaired-of mass audience have had no experience with anything but trivia, but given the chance might choose the better.

Of the value and cultural influence of radio and television there is considerable difference of opinion; of their economic importance there can be no question. When television started to grow, there were many predictions that the end of the radio was in sight. Actually, of course, this is far from true. The character of the sets has changed. No one buys big radios; instead they buy several little ones. The type of program has changed too, so that today radio programs consist largely of disc jockeys and news; but the radio is a firmly fixed part of our culture and our economy. Over 15 million radio sets were produced in 1957 and were sold at wholesale for 374 million dollars. Advertisers still found it worthwhile to invest 623 million dollars in radio advertising during 1957.

In every way, television outstrips radio—in money spent for original equipment, in the time spent with it, in attacks on it by sociologists, in the size of the audience it reaches, and in the money spent on advertising. Approximately 80 per cent of all American families own television sets. According to an A.C. Nielson report, the television set in the average home runs more than six hours a day.

A quick summary of the industry's statistics should complete the picture of its size and influence. In 1957 television production exceeded 6 million sets valued at 833 million dollars. Radio and television repairs took 652 million dollars of consumers' expenditures. Indirectly, as soon as a man buys a television set, he becomes a part of a rating which does much to make or break a television program. Thus he has a hand in controlling the volume of advertising which in 1957 reached 1.3 billion dollars. This total was exceeded only by newspaper advertising.

Two other mass media must be added to the list. In 1957 consumers spent just over 1 billion dollars for movie admissions and 378 million dollars for phonograph records. The growth of the record business, more than that of any of the other mass media, is due to the rising interest in "elite culture."

Minorities Count

What are the conclusions to be drawn from this consideration of the economics of mass culture? It has often been said, in relation to our position of leadership in the world today, that power carries with it responsibility. This is as true for the business community as it is for the nation. We need not decide whether the mass media and Madison Avenue actually create all of the consumer's standards and requirements, but I think no one will argue with the thesis that they have a major influence.

Let us take an illustration. Even before Sputnik I, spokesmen for industry were continually complaining that we do not have enough scientists. Since that first Sputnik, the cry has become a wail. A survey among youngsters indicated that few were interested in becoming scientists and thought them cold and inhuman. Isn't this concept at least encouraged by the television programs—commercially sponsored—which use the stereotype of the scientist—brilliant, cold, aware of time only as the fourth dimension, loving his science more than his wife and his dog?

There is an unfortunate tendency to accept unques-

tioningly all the popular statements about the consumer
—or, in the case of mass media, about the audience. For
example, we are told that the average American adult
has a 13-year-old mentality or, the picture of a sufficiently undressed girl can sell anything from plumbing
to books. Even if such statements have some foundation
in fact, disregarding the mature segment of the audience,
or the people who are interested in the contents of a
book, means leaving a valuable part of the market untapped.

Averages are a little like chopped meat. After it's
ground up, we don't know much about what went into
it. No research, educational, economic, or social, can
afford to neglect the extremes and disregard minority
opinions. Averages are only a statistical convenience;
average people are hard to find.

In 1946 Mentor paperbacks were considered "high-
brow," and many distributors wouldn't touch them. Today they are distributed in quantities of 100,000. Although the growth in higher education helped create
some of the market for better paperbacks, the bulk of it
was there waiting to be satisfied.

A second illustration, also taken from the paperback
industry, concerns the covers they used. In the belief
that the mass market would be willing to buy anything
as long as the cover pictured a girl in a compromising
situation with torn clothes, the publishers of paperbacks
used this kind of cover for any book with a girl in it. And
most books do have girls in them, even if they are cooks
and the book is a cookbook. But the publishers underestimated the public taste, or at least part of it, and now
must overcome the feeling which many people still have
that a paperback book is trash. Today the covers are
more honest. Sensational covers are confined to sensa-

tional books, and frequently even these are toned down. *Peyton Place*, which could honestly have claimed a "hot" cover, was published in a sober, dignified jacket.

Industry has generally found that research pays off. Market research aimed at breaking down the "typical" member of the audience into its component parts could be economically rewarding.

Elite Culture

The fine arts are generally not distributed through mass media, and there is no question of big business pressure. For many of our serious artists today, the problem is economic survival. We have this contradiction today in America: while the interest and demand for the creative and performing arts are growing, the economic position of the artist remains low. Starving in a garret is out of style. Even if the poet does not covet his neighbor's Cadillac, he does like to eat.

How popular have the "unpopular arts" become?

In literature, as I have cited before, there is a rapid rise in sales of the higher-priced paperbacks, especially aimed at educated readers.

In music the record is just as striking. Let me quote from a study made for UNESCO by Arnold Walter, Director of the Royal Conservatory of Music in Toronto:

> No doubt musical America was once (and not so long ago) a colony of Europe. Performers and educators, the musical repertory and music education methods had to be imported. Orchestral concerts and opera performances were more a luxury for the well-to-do than a spiritual necessity for the common man, a social pastime rather than a religious experience. But this is now a thing of the past. America's contribution to literature, to painting and architecture is no small one; but it is music which is first and foremost of the arts.

All phases of music have participated in this growth. Take the growth of the orchestra, for example. In 1900 there were 4 established symphony orchestras in the United States. Today there are 31 major orchestras (those which employ musicians at a regular weekly salary for a specified number of weeks per season) and 140 second symphony orchestras (those in which the musicians are engaged on a per concert basis). Orchestral groups are appearing in towns of 4,000 or 5,000 population. To these groups should be added the numerous school and amateur orchestras, which probably number several hundred and are found in all parts of the country.

Attendance at concerts doubled between 1940 and 1955. The spread of serious music interest in the United States can also be seen in the work of countless music clubs, the development of community concerts, the increase in the number of small opera companies, the millions of listeners who attended faithfully the concerts of the NBC Orchestra, and the extensive program of music education carried on by the universities both for vocational and avocational training. Musical training and musical experience is provided through orchestras, choruses, bands, and glee clubs. To quote Arnold Walter again, ". . . it can truthfully be said that during the last three decades music education in America progressed faster and further than anywhere else at any time in history."

High-fidelity recording has certainly shared in the growth of serious music; the introduction of stereo will give it further impetus. Although there is nothing to preclude the use of high-fidelity equipment for "rock-and-roll" music, it is safe to assume that most people buy it for serious use. In the last five years, sales of audio components (speakers, amplifiers, tape recorders, tuners, and record changers) have risen by more than 300 per cent. "Packaged" high-fidelity equipment sales had soared to 335 million dollars when this phase of the industry was only 4 years old.

Record sales in 1957 were around 378 million dollars, higher than the 1956 total, which had been labeled "huge" by the Record Industry Association of America. Both "pop" and classical records shared in the increase, but classical and opera records have been among the leaders in expanding sales.

What of the other cultural forms? Everywhere there is a broadening interest and a less selected audience. In 1933, when Hurok first brought over the original Ballet de Monte Carlo, the venture was a financial fiasco. There was a recital when sixteen people constituted the audience. It's true that we were in the middle of a terrible economic crisis, but prices were low and certainly there was much to escape from in everyday living. In the intervening years the situation has been completely reversed. Today, when the Royal Ballet performs, it is completely sold out. In addition, there are three major American ballet companies where none existed fifty years ago.

The dance, as an art form, now appeals to a broader audience. Hurok has found that the most popular recitals are the full-length classical ballets. They offer costumes, a story, familiar rhythms, and in general are easily understood and appreciated by an audience just becoming aware of the dance as an art form. On the other hand, a Pittsburgh television station re-ran, by popular request, a film by Martha Graham on the modern dance.

The wider public interest in painting and sculpture is

another illustration of the cultural awakening. Although
the acquisition of masterpieces is still the province of
millionaires and museums, attendance at art galleries
and museums has jumped to about 55 million visitors a
year. An exhibit of Picasso's work at the Museum of
Modern Art in New York drew a record crowd of more
than 200,000 people. The number of museums has
quadrupled in the last twenty-five years. More moder-
ately priced art works and good reproductions are being
sold.

Art, as well as music, has benefited from the trend
away from specialization in education. More appreciation of art is being included in all school curricula, from
the public school through the university. Nor should we
overlook the numerous adult-education programs, which
for a minimal fee encourage the housewife and the
businessman to try oil painting, sketching, short story
writing, community singing, and even opera.

How do we, as a society, pay our performing and
creative artists? Let me illustrate with two examples—
the poets, a comparatively small group who have found
a comparatively satisfactory economic solution, and the
musicians, a large group whose economic position has
been steadily deteriorating.

Poetry is certainly not a commercial product in the
United States, or is poetry widely enough circulated to
make publishing profitable. The general public will not
adopt and support the poet, even in today's improved
cultural atmosphere, but the universities have. The
arrangement by which the poet serves on the university
staff and the university publishes his work through their
own press is mutually profitable. The poet is assured of
some economic security and the opportunity of having
his work published. The university, although probably

losing money on the publishing venture, can thus attract
some choice members to its staff.

No such relatively good solution has been found for
the musician. As a group, they are a "depressed" class.
In testimony before the Forand Subcommittee on Excise
Taxes, Dr. Robert C. Shook, Vice-president of the International Statistical Bureau, Inc., summed up the situation thus:

> It is a distressing and little-known fact that the economic
> position of musicians, even though they are practitioners of
> one of the highest cultural art forms, has shown nothing but
> a steady deterioration.
>
> Music is the product of the musician's talent and training;
> and music, through the media of high-fidelity recording,
> electrical transcription, and radio and television broadcast-
> ing, has an audience many times greater than it had twenty
> years ago. But the individual musician who looks to music
> as a means of support is much worse off today than he was
> twenty years ago, or ten years ago, or even last year—worse
> off, perhaps, than at any time in all history.
>
> Most musicians cannot expect to find a full-time job, since
> so few exist. They can hope to work full-time, as musicians,
> only by the risky and discouraging process of finding a
> never-ending succession of part-time jobs.

In an analysis of the work available to musicians and
presented in this same testimony, it was shown that less
than 10 per cent of available jobs would have provided
an annual income of more than $3,000 a year. It is no
cause for wonder that musicians do not want their children to become musicians.

The two main causes for the desperate economic
situation of the musicians are the technological advances
which have largely substituted "canned" for "live" music and the 20 per cent "cabaret" tax, which discourages
the use of live orchestras in restaurants. The first of
these causes—technology—is a permanent development,

but the second—the tax—can be eliminated. In this case the power to tax has proved to be the power to destroy the musician, although it was surely not so intended by the framers of the tax law.

In another case the tax laws have operated for the benefit of the museums and the general public. When a painting is sold at a profit in the United States, the seller must pay a capital gains tax. Not so in Europe. As a result, the active market in masterpieces has migrated abroad. On the other hand, when a collector buys a work of art, which he doesn't intend to sell, he frequently donates it to a museum, retaining only some form of life ownership. He may then deduct the amount of the purchase from his taxable income, but if he retained outright ownership he could not claim it as a deduction. In addition, if he left the painting to his children, he would also leave them the burden of paying the inheritance tax, which could run as high as 80 to 90 per cent of the original value of the painting. The family would thus have paid twice for the same work of art.

Who Are the New Patrons?

These illustrations of the effects of the tax laws brings up the whole question of the proper role of government in the encouragement of art. What part can it play in finding a solution for the underpaid and underemployed musician, for the symphony orchestras operating with deficits each year, the opera companies that must make special appeals to keep alive, the little theatre groups and dance groups that could bring the best art forms to all parts of the United States?

If we do not find a solution, the cultural awakening will die for lack of performing artists. We must find new angels to take the place of the millionaires whose ranks have been depleted by taxes. We must look to three sources, corporations, foundations, and the government. All three show promise.

In recent years industry has realized that the narrowly educated individual does not make a good executive, that technical knowledge is not enough. In line with this new thought large corporations have been helping to support the universities and have set up their own programs to encourage employees to study the humanities and arts and to participate actively in choral groups, small orchestras, and art classes.

Corporate support for education, both in direct grants to universities and in the form of scholarships, has been well established during the last ten years, but direct support of the creative arts is relatively new. In many cases the reasons for this support come under the heading of "enlightened self-interest." The two most often given are the attempt to revive declining downtown areas by making them centers where the best in entertainment and the arts are available and the attempt to attract the cream of technical and executive personnel, who look for cultural advantages for the children in addition to a good school system and salary.

The largest privately financed cultural construction program is currently being planned for Lincoln Center in New York City. When finished, it is expected to house opera, symphonies, drama, dance, and other performing arts. The total cost will run around 75 million dollars, and 10 per cent of this amount is expected to come from corporations.

This is a relatively new departure in corporate gift giving. Until now, only about one per cent of corporate gifts have been going to the arts, and the new development will be closely watched for its effects on commerce as well as culture. Cities as widely separated as Pittsburgh, Boston, Winston-Salem, Ft. Wayne, and Cincinnati are planning civic auditoriums for art performances and promoting art festivals which are expected to attract vacationing visitors with money to spend.

The fact that a good part of corporate support to art will be for business' sake rather than only for art's sake and that urban rebuilders can see in cultural centers an attraction strong enough to halt the decay of downtown areas is the best evidence that the cultural resurgence in America is widespread and growing. Individual business men may give donations to causes with no thought of profit, but corporations are in the habit of expecting some return for their money even though it may be indirect and as intangible as goodwill.

In a different class are the tax-free foundations, the new millionaires created for the benevolent purpose of giving away money. Three foundations have contributed 15.5 million dollars to Lincoln Center in New York City, and the Ford Foundation, one of the giants, has given its first five grants to the performing arts, three for music, one for art, and one for drama. More important, the Foundation will spend $400,000 in the next two years on a survey to determine the financial needs of the performing arts and how they can best be met. The first grants totaling $760,000 are just the beginning.

Several points in the Ford grant should be emphasized. First, there is encouragement for American work. Second, it recognizes the need to develop individual talents which might otherwise be lost for lack of financial aid. Third, it recognizes that the arts should be available to all people, not just those near the great cultural centers. The aim of the grant for drama is to establish a repertory company which will tour the small towns of the Middle West.

The third part of the solution lies in financial support from the federal government, that is, some form of subsidy, although many business and cultural leaders hope to avoid it. The idea of federal support for essential parts of our national life is certainly not new. When necessary, the government has helped support agriculture, transportation, scientific research, and education. It has even given financial aid for rebuilding opera houses and concert halls abroad.

Europe has long recognized the need for public support of the fine arts. Audience attendance has never been able to support a symphony orchestra. The famous opera companies of Europe, with their symphonies and ballets, receive government aid. The list is impressive and should answer the question of whether state-supported art is necessarily nationalized or standardized. It includes Milan, Vienna, Berlin, Paris, and London. France gives support to four national theatres, five symphony orchestras, and many provincial theatres. In Mexico the Ministry of Fine Arts supports a National School of Music, an opera company, a ballet theatre, and a national symphony. In Australia every province has a state-supported orchestra.

In the United States the obligation of governmental support is being recognized and fulfilled by many state and city governments. Vermont, Massachusetts, Rhode Island, Arkansas, and North Carolina grant funds for the support of symphony orchestras. Philadelphia sets aside $50,000 to help support the Philadelphia Symphony. Sioux City, Iowa, has levied a special orchestra tax. The American cities giving art grants are geographically scattered and varied in size.

The federal government is far behind. Only once in our history has there been a real effort to aid the creative artist, but it took the tragedy of the Great Depression to stimulate it; and with the end of the depression it disappeared. Artists were not just given a dole on which to live; they were given the opportunity of working in their own specialized fields. Although the WPA was ridiculed and criticized, it spread beauty in many forms and saved the talent of many creative artists.

Fortunately there is a growing movement in official Washington for federal aid to encourage performing artists. Legislation has been backed by such prominent senators as Humphrey, Lehman, Kefauver, Javits, Morse, and Fullbright. The bills speak of the plight of the professional musician and the need to support the culture upon which our civilization is founded.

In May, 1957, Senator Javits of New York introduced a bill to establish a United States Arts Foundation as an independent agency in the executive branch of the federal government. In introducing the bill Senator Javits said:

It is especially appropriate that this legislation be proposed at this time when the battle of the budget is at a high level, because economy also implies wisdom in making expenditures. In the proposed establishment of a United States Art Foundation, we are in an area of comparatively small expenditure—from 3 million to 5 million dollars—that gives great impetus to private activities of many times that amount and will afford pleasure to vast areas of the country in seeing the performing arts now denied them. We have done without this for too long—considering that other peoples, not nearly as wealthy as we, have had comparable organization for years. We have only ourselves to blame if we don't take advantage of our own culture.

The bill provides for the establishment of a board to encourage and stimulate the study and advancement of the performing arts and the public interest in them. Loans may be made to any professional group, or any educational group meeting standards prescribed by the Foundation, engaged in the performing arts or in instruction work in connection with them. Financial assistance would be provided only to nonprofit enterprises.

More recently, Senator Fullbright introduced two bills intended to increase government participation in the arts, one to establish a National Capital Center for the performing arts in Washington and the second to permit the government to collect royalties on all music in public domain and use the money "to encourage the creation, understanding and appreciation of music."

It may seem to the purist that the senator's reason for advocating government support so that "we will not hang our heads in shame whenever people tell us about the Bolshoi Theatre" is the wrong one, but it fits in well with our new national attitude of "keeping up with the Russians" and may work better as a prod than Senator Javits' more fundamental reasons.

One concrete achievement in the right direction is the Library Services Act, signed by President Eisenhower in June 1956. It is designed to promote the development of public library services in rural areas which do not have adequate facilities. It authorizes Congress to appropriate 7.5 million dollars a year for a five-year period, to be allocated to states on a matching fund basis.

During the first year under the act, Congress appropriated only 2.5 million dollars for its implementation. For the second year the appropriation was 5 million dollars. In 1958 the appropriation will be higher but still below the authorized level.

So pressing is the need for this phase of public education, that even with these restricted funds, 49 out of 53 states and territories started programs under the provisions of the act, on a matching fund basis. Unless the full amount is provided in the two remaining years of the act's life, the efforts already underway will prove abortive, and 27 million Americans will continue without this most basic cultural service.

It would seem that the richest country in the world cannot afford 7.5 million dollars a year for library services. By contrast, Great Britain, even during the austerity of the postwar years, supported the Old Vic, Covent Garden, the BBC symphony, the National Ballet, and the Shakespearean theatres with public funds.

The totalitarian states took as their motto "Guns before Butter." As a nation we have guns and butter, but we must also have artists, musicians, and writers. We claim world leadership. In material achievements the claim is uncontested. We have the best indoor plumbing, the greatest number of telephones, and the highest per capita income. We are envied and sometimes hated for our wealth. But if we are mature enough to produce and support a culture that truly reflects our society and ideals, perhaps we can speak more effectively through it to the peoples of the world.

"The arts," said Franklin Delano Roosevelt, ". . . inspire a fervor for spiritual values . . . and strengthen democracy against those forces which would subjugate mankind . . . make us aware of the common humanity which is ours and shall one day unite the nations of the world in a great brotherhood."

6

SUBURBIA

Urbia—Sub, Ex, and Inter

Since the earliest days of the first colonial settlements Americans have been on the move—mining, leveling, planting, irrigating, founding towns and deserting them, discovering forests and depleting them, seeking a place to live, a fortune in gold, or a new opportunity—in many ways changing the face of the land. We are still moving today and changing the face of the land. We meet no Indians and seek no gold mines, but as the growing population spreads from the core of the city to its fringes, from the fringes past the city line to the suburbs, and then keeps on going, the open areas, cultivated or uncultivated, yield to the developer and the highway engineer. The potato farm is replaced by five hundred houses; the air above is crisscrossed with wires, and the ground below is crisscrossed with sewers. Since the war ended and civilian building really got started again, approximately a million acres of rural land have been diverted to urban and related nonagricultural uses each year.

The concentration of our population in urban areas has been going on at a rapid pace for more than a hundred years. As industry rather than farming came to dominate the economy, and as the standard of living rose and came to include a need for services as well as things, the city attracted migrants and immigrants with its opportunities for varied employment, potential wealth, and cultural amenities. Between 1840 and 1930 the proportion of our total population living in urban areas rose from 11 per cent to 56 per cent. The depression of the 1930's and the war in the 1940's brought an abrupt halt to this long-term migration, leaving the pressures which were behind it to build up and explode when the war ended.

The explosion had its center in the city, but like all explosions in this high-powered age, the effects were felt far out from the center, in the thinly settled suburbs. Until this time a house in the suburbs or country was reserved for the wealthy or at least for the upper-middle class. Now it became the mecca for the growing middle class.

The end of the war ushered in a new era of growth and prosperity which made the depression of the 1930's a nightmare to be pushed back into the subconscious mind of the public. Economic activity was high, the marriage rate was almost double the depression rate, and incomes were rising. Millions of families advanced to income brackets where they could afford good housing, but there was practically none available. Returning service men and their wives took whatever they could get and still, two or three years after the war ended, there were probably 2.5 million families living with relatives. There just were not enough houses or apartments to go around.

The housing boom which got underway to meet this desperate need was centered outside the cities, first nearby, but gradually going farther and farther out. Here there was land readily available and, compared to land in the city, it was cheap. Building costs had sky-rocketed but could be partly offset by the economies of mass production on large tracts of cheap land. Federal aid in the form of Veterans Administration and Federal Housing Authority mortgages kept the down payments small and the interest rates low. Automobiles and gasoline were again available to serve as daily transportation to work or to public transportation. The five-day week made a long trip to work less burdensome.

For the young family living with relatives or in sub-standard dwellings there was little choice. For the growing family with inadequate space there was also little choice. Even for the family with adequate space by prewar standards the pressures to get the children out of the city were accumulating—the crime rate was high, schools were on double or triple session, play space was inadequate, and the child-rearing experts were in agreement that "the city is no place to raise a child."

The developments were built, sold, and occupied in record time, frequently with the streets still unpaved, police protection not supplied, fire boxes not yet provided.

Almost a million families a year have been joining the majority who own their own homes. (The banks who hold the mortgages must think this a strange delusion.) Latest data show the total at almost 60 per cent of all families. Most of the increase has been in the suburban areas of standard metropolitan districts. Between 1950 and 1955 the increase of population in the suburbs was four times the increase in the population in central cities.

. or the novice homeowner there were many unpleasant surprises in store. The good earth turned out to be sand on Long Island, clay in Maryland, rocks in Connecticut. The builder's idea of a fully landscaped plot was a sad collection of wilted shrubs and flourishing weeds; the grass grew easily only in the flower beds. Carefully calculated budgets became rapidly obsolete in the face of rising taxes for the new, shiny schools and the family's own rising ideas of what it needed. The blissful (and inexpensive) picture of the family spending the summer together in the back yard was frequently disrupted by the realization that the children's "peers" were going to get their "group experiences" in camp. "Doing-it-yourself" was not as simple as the book said and could end up by one's calling in the plumber and paying twice as much as if he had never tried.

Despite these, and more serious problems, the return from the suburbs is only a trickle compared with the continuing outbound flow. Unmarried people, the childless couple, and the older couple whose children are married may find that they do not fit into the suburban community, or that its disadvantages outweigh its advantages. But for the millions of middle-income families with growing children the city has very little decent living space. To many the city means noise, dirt, overcrowding, and crime rather than concerts, museums, and art galleries. It has become a place for the very poor who live in slums or public housing developments or for the very rich who can afford the best of the old or new housing. Most so-called middle-income housing is too expensive for middle-income families, and if they end up by paying as much or slightly more for the house in the suburbs with its added expenses for commuting and grass seed, at least they have more room for living and playing, and less worry about the children being on the streets.

In a study made by David Riesman of the Center for the Study of Leisure, at the University of Chicago, on the hopes and ambitions of several hundred college seniors it was found that "Those who hailed originally from the suburbs suffered from no disenchantment and wanted to return to them—often to the same one—while both city-bred and small town boys also preferred the suburbs."

It may therefore come as a surprise to many fairly well-satisfied suburbanites that according to popular books and newspaper articles they and their communities are the source and center of all kinds of evils, that they are homogenized, excessively conformist, live in potential slums, see, hear, and know nothing beyond their picture windows, belong to too many organizations, are dominated by the children who practically never see their fathers. If they live in exurbia, the home of the "V.I.P." made famous by Spectorsky, they have high I.Q.s, high incomes, higher expenditures, even higher liquor consumption, and a high rate of exchange for minks, maids, and wives.

If the suburbanite sees life through a picture window, many of his appraisers see life in the suburbs through the keyhole; the view may be sensational but it's always very narrow. The failures and ironies of suburban living are all too obvious and easily exaggerated into "good copy." It would seem that by crossing the city line we enter a new and different world; actually, many of the most criticized characteristics are neither new nor so different.

Conformity

No article or discussion of life in the suburbs fails to emphasize conformity—of dress, furnishings, routine, and thought.

The houses are all alike. Blame it on the builders; the buyers had no choice. After a few years they are not that much alike any more. Pieces have been added, and the harsh outlines are softened by trees and shrubs.

Every one has a barbecue grill in the back yard. It's really quite convenient. The mess is blown away by the breeze, and it's much easier to reach than the picnic grounds which are separated from home by clogged roads.

The television antenna is an unvarying high point on the roof. People in the city watch television too, but nobody watches them for publication purposes.

All the children wear blue jeans. Why not? They are sturdy, washable, and respectable, even though disreputable-looking. What more could a mother expect of children's clothes? In any case, children everywhere wear what "all the kids are wearing."

Everybody watches their neighbors to know just how much to buy of what. The phrase "keeping up with the Joneses" goes back a long time before the suburbs grew to their present importance, and whether the middle-class suburban family keeps up with, down with, or on a level with the Joneses, it is only following a long established American custom.

In 1910 Mrs. Cornelius Vanderbilt started a fad by wearing a diamond-studded "headache" band. The rest of society followed, substituting fabric for diamonds when necessary. In *Patterns of Culture*, published in 1934, (by Houghton Mifflin) Ruth Benedict said of

American middle-class values, ". . . houses are built and clothing bought and entertainments attended that each family may prove that it has not been left out of the game . . . individual choices and direct satisfactions are reduced to a minimum and conformity is sought beyond all other human gratifications." Conformity was not born in the look-alike development house of the suburbs. The small town of fifty years ago (which seems to be becoming more ideal the further in time it recedes) was a center of the most rigid conformity.

The worst kind of conformity which afflicts us today, however, in and out of suburbia, is conformity of thought and expressed opinions. One does not have to wear a toga in Times Square to be an individualist; in fact being a Bohemian in dress and manners can become just as narrow a pattern of conformity as slacks and sport shirt in the back yard.

The big push toward mental uniformity came from both psychology and politics. For years educational psychologists' stressing of "adjustment" and "group experiences" has sandpapered off the square pegs. To attribute conformity to development housing and forget the extreme measures taken in the name of national security is ridiculous and dangerous. When a book in a private home was removed from the bookshelf to the closet because the author or the book club was on a list, when a friend was fired from a nonsensitive job because he was so foolish as to pick Communists for parents, when the government security agent came asking about a neighbor "What does he read? What newspapers have you seen in his house? Have you discussed politics?" When the net reached out not only for the big fish who might fight back but also for the little sardines who didn't know which way to turn—then was conformity nourished.

Surely there is conformity in the suburbs, but where are there great numbers of nonconformists? If a middle-class suburbanite suffers from lack of individuality and an overwhelming desire to be just "one of the boys" it is because this is one of the strongest pressures in American life, not because he lives in the suburbs.

Homogenized and Child-Centered

It is said that families in the suburbs are all the same in age, income, education, and occupation, and that growing children get a very narrow experience. To some extent this is truer for the suburb than for the city. There are few elderly people, few low-income families, and few millionaires in the suburbs. The top and the bottom of the population distribution are shorn off, but the band that remains is wider than frequently implied. The range of organizations that flourishes in the suburbs and the varied list of courses offered in the adult education programs are evidence that not all the residents think alike or are interested in the same subjects.

The advantages of the city in this respect are often more apparent than real. The city may house a great variety of people different in income, religion, color, national origin, and customs, but a child growing up in a particular neighborhood may have contact with as little variety as the child in the suburbs. Neither public nor private housing is built to accommodate the very rich and the very poor. In New York City there are areas where slums are around the corner from some of the most exclusive houses, but the occupants of each go their separate ways and the children go to their separate schools.

The leveling process for income, tastes, and backgrounds has been going on for the whole country, not for just the suburbs. Immigration from a variety of foreign lands has all but stopped. Education through high school is commonplace, and special training is necessary for many lines of work. The income distribution is more and more heavily weighted in the middle brackets, with fewer very poor families and fewer millionaires.

It comes as a shock to some observers that life in the suburbs is child-centered, that mothers spend so much of their time den-mothering, chauffering and class-mothering, that their conversation runs strongly in the direction of toilet training and the Freudian implications of thumb sucking, and that even father is embroiled in the Little League and school committees. Can it be simply because there are so many children in the suburbs, and that long ago it was decreed that children were to be heard as well as seen?

Would these same mothers, if living in the city, be more likely to discuss foreign policy than feeding problems? Would they be leaving the dishes in the sink, the children unaccounted for, and the shopping undone to spend a pleasant day in the museum or at a matinee? It is an established fact of life that where there are children life is likely to be child-centered.

It is also fairly well established that fathers must regularly leave the women and children and earn the family's bread, butter, and television set, whether they live in the city or a suburb. This leaves mother with the discipline problem, which seems to dismay some observers of suburbia. Punishment (say the experts) must be administered when the crime is committed. Would mother really say "Wait till Papa gets home," if papa was expected at six o'clock instead of at seven?

The suburbs are oversocialized and overorganized. In the early stages they probably are, but after a few years the socializing and organization joining become more selective. There are all kinds of problems in a new community—recreation programs, school taxes, flooded streets, insufficient traffic lights—and the former resident of a big city is encouraged to join by the feeling that in this small community his voice will have meaning too.

The Real Problems

The danger of this shallow criticism is that it tends to draw attention away from the very real and long-term problems which confront the suburbs and their core cities, problems which must be solved not in opposition to each other, but in unity. The important research on urban problems being undertaken by our major universities, the attempts to foster planning instead of growth alone, the importance to each suburban resident of the use to which the surrounding land is put, the impending decisions concerning location of the new highways: these items are reserved for reading by specialists. Meanwhile the general public is left with the feeling that the big problem of suburban growth is whether the automatic dryer or the sports car is the new status symbol in suburbia.

Suburbanites find that many of the city's problems that they hoped to escape move with them to the suburbs in altered form. Race tensions and religious prejudice are not exclusive to the city slums, nor are they eliminated by the deeds to new houses with illegal restrictive clauses on resale. The sale of a house in Levittown, Pennsylvania, to a Negro family caused a nationally publicized community battle. Only locally

publicized are the conflicts over the celebration of religious holidays in the public schools or the bitter tax
struggles with the older, local population whose children
are out of school or do not use the public schools, but
who are suddenly taxed for the new schools that the in-
coming children must have.

The problem of adequate schooling is not automatically solved by moving out of the city. Parents who have
voted to tax themselves beyond their financial means to
avoid the double and triple sessions of the city schools
often find that handsome buildings do not make a school.
Curriculums, teacher training, and educational theory
may have been successfully geared to a small static
community, but they may fail to accommodate the needs
of a larger group with more varied backgrounds and
abilities. In this connection, it is interesting to note that
Columbia University's Teachers College has undertaken
a study, which may run as long as five years, aimed at
"identifying and alleviating some of the social and educational problems confronting changing suburban communities."

Paradoxically, recreation is becoming a problem of
suburban living. Recreation for small children can be
pleasantly and inexpensively provided in the back yard,
but children grow up and even parents eventually find
time for something besides gardening and puttering.
Teen-age recreation is too often organized around the
church and temple. Tremendous tracts of land have
been swallowed up for housing developments with little
or no provision made for tennis courts, golf courses,
swimming pools, and baseball fields. Along the coasts
and the lakes, the waterfronts are being bought and
closed off for private use with the result that in some

sections, notably the New York metropolitan area, the
public facilities are already overcrowded, and some communities have closed their facilities to all but their own
residents.

As the areas built up for housing spread further, the
residents will find even the overcrowded facilities inac-
cessible. The highways are already so jammed on a
sunny Sunday that a few hours at a recreation area may
require an equivalent number of hours in traveling. The
spectacular increase in car ownership since the war, so
that now we have 69 million cars on the road, has resulted in the spectacle of 200 horsepower vehicles moving with the speed of a one horsepower buggy.

Recreation facilities and the preservation of undeveloped green acres are only part of the problem of land
use. Truck farming, normally carried on intensively on
the outskirts of the cities, has been giving way to housing
developments with no regard to best economic use for
the land. The farmer makes a profit on his land, the
builder on his houses, but what will be the effect on food
prices and supplies? Will it take an expensive development program to reclaim other land that is less suitable
for this kind of farming? If the residential building program had been planned instead of pushed, perhaps an
area could have been left for the farm, with profit to
the beauty and economy of the community. In one
place it is the farm, in another the citrus grove, and in
another the last bit of woodland, but once gone it cannot
be recreated.

The speculative builder puts up his houses where
building is most profitable, not where living will be best.
There are few controls which oblige him to make provision for parks or even industrial centers, which could

provide jobs near home and tax revenues to support the
desperately needed schools. There have been attempts
at control through zoning—in California, for example,
where suburban growth has been phenomenal—but generally there has been too much conflict of interest among
the groups who must work together. The immediate
profit to be taken from skyrocketing land values and
building has precluded much consideration of the long-
term results.

The Federal Highway Act, passed in 1956, can either
encourage planning and rational land use or continue
the uneconomic and unaesthetic development which has
been so well characterized as "urban sprawl." The Act
provides for the construction of 41,000 miles of roads
within fifteen years. This interstate network is to be
planned to meet the traffic needs of 1975, and it is hoped
that with this construction it will be possible for people
and goods to move freely in metropolitan areas, from
the core city to the suburbs and from suburb to suburb.

In the opinion of the President's Advisory Committee,
which drew up the program, the highway system will
help "disperse our factories, our stores, our people; in
short, to create a revolution in living habits." Despite
this recognition of the far-reaching effects on America's
future pattern for living, the standards for the roads
have been left to state and federal highway engineers
to set, and it is reasonable to expect that good engineering practice rather than future good living will determine where the new roads are laid. In providing the
straightest and shortest distance between two points we
will have achieved little of lasting value if we also encourage additional congestion in already congested areas
or preempt land suited best for food production.

An impressive illustration by William H. Whyte Jr.,

is given in his thorough discussion of this problem. Santa Clara County in California managed, in 1954, to put through a zoning act designed to preserve part of their valley for farming in the face of an enveloping home development wave. But as soon as this was accomplished the people discovered that the state was planning a new highway which would run right through the valley floor. They pointed out that by adding some mileage to the road it would be possible to run it at the edge of the foothills and preserve the valley for farming and as one of the few remaining green open spaces in the area. The engineers had to think about it.

The location of the highways, and particularly their interchange points, will have as direct a bearing on urban development as did the river and railway junction in the past. One illustration will serve to highlight this obvious but important fact. A tremendous shopping center is planned for New Rochelle, New York. The center will be known as the Westchester Terminal Plaza, will cost 41 million dollars, and should be completed in about two years. The location is significant. It adjoins the New Rochelle interchange of the New England Thruway and is alongside an already approved arterial highway which will provide approaches from the Thruway and the municipal area.

As Mr. Whyte points out, there are means available, without creating new powers and government, by which the state can buy land or land rights in order to preserve undeveloped areas and farmlands. But unless the interested groups discover that they have more common aims than differences, the roads will have been built and irreplaceable beauty destroyed with the communities involved having little to say.

Metropolitan Government

The big problem in urban-suburban government today is that the issues have outgrown the multiplicity of
small government units. The traditional organization of
government into four levels, municipal, county, state,
and federal, no longer describes realistically the way in
which people live and work or the manner in which our
network of roads and suburban development have created common problems for politically divided territories.

The central city must supply services for people who
earn their living there during the day and leave in the
evening to live and pay taxes elsewhere. The suburbs,
already growing into cities themselves, are afraid that
their interests will be overwhelmed if considered at the
same time as the big city's. The farm areas, which influence our state governments out of all proportion to
their population importance, look unsympathetically
upon both the city and suburb.

The result has been a kind of land-grabbing, with mu-
nicipalities annexing property with as little plan as the
developers build houses. The boundary lines may run
through the middle of streets, with neighbors paying
different taxes to different communities and getting a
different quality of services in return. One community,
practically all new and all residential, may have great
difficulty in providing for basic fire, police, and educational needs. A neighboring community, which includes
a large industrial plant can provide excellent services.

Small communities which have limited financial resources, whose citizens concentrate their interest on the
local schools and tax rate, cannot handle the problems
which do not stop at the boundary line. Crime creeps
over the border, waste disposal is uneconomical and

inefficient if provided for only locally, water supplies have to be divided, waterfront areas must be developed with more than the immediate vicinity in mind, and above all, highways and traffic control must be considered from the widest possible angle—the whole metropolitan region, lest a bad clot in one area affect the whole body.

The suburbs have long considered themselves as attached only to the central city but this concept is becoming outdated. The suburbs are related not only to their core cities but to each other, and transportation facilities will have to catch up with this new status. Highway systems radiating out from a center are inadequate, and part of urban congestion is caused by the fact that the city provides the only route by which to go from suburb to suburb. The importance of "ring" roads was illustrated in the Boston metropolitan area where the development of Route 128 around portions of the region resulted in a rapid and unexpected increase in industrial plant location and traffic. In four years over 100 million dollars' worth of nonresidential building went up.

The consideration of the traffic problem must not only transcend area subdivisions, but also must take account of public as well as private transportation means and parking facilities. A mass of automobiles converging on a city, even by way of the finest network of roads, would be purposeless unless there was adequate provision for leaving the car and moving freely within the city.

Two possible solutions to the problem of too many small governments are most frequently suggested. The first involves the creation of a new strata of administration, a "metropolitan government" which would collect all the taxes, do all the planning, and provide all the services for the metropolitan area. This is being tried

successfully in Canada, where Ontario set up Metropolitan Toronto, cutting across municipality divisions to
achieve more efficient functioning. The central govern-
ing body includes the Mayor of Toronto, the mayors of
twelve suburban communities and eleven members of
the Toronto City Council. Its powers are limited to
functions best carried out by a "super government" but
are effective for the whole area.

In the United States, a pioneering attempt is being
made in Florida. By a narrow voting margin, the government of Dade County was reorganized to act as a
central authority for Miami and its satellite communities. The reorganization is still too new, however, to be
able to judge its effectiveness. Reorganization plans and
metropolitan governments have also been proposed for
Seattle, Pittsburgh, Sacramento, and Nashville.

One difficulty blocking the formation of metropolitan
governments is the fact that the state—made up of mu-
nicipalities—must pass enabling legislation. On a small
scale, this is about as easy as convincing individual
countries to renounce part of their autonomy in favor of
a world government.

A second solution is the creation of special authorities
or districts to deal with individual metropolitan problems. One advantage of this method is that it has already demonstrated its ability to cut across state lines as
well as across municipal boundaries. A notable example
is the Port of New York Authority which successfully
operates harbor facilities, tunnels, bridges, and airports
for New York and New Jersey. Whatever advantages
and disadvantages this plan may have, it is sometimes
the only one which can achieve a required objective
within a given time. In the Philadelphia and San Fran-

cisco Bay areas, special authorities were recommended to handle transportation policies although, at the same time, it was recognized that a limited metropolitan government would have been better.

A judgment on the best policy cannot be made for all metropolitan areas in the country. The solution will have to be worked out on the basis of individual area needs. The need is not so much to decide which solution is best, but rather to educate the citizens involved to the fact that there is a problem, that small interests cannot answer big questions, and that the extension of the highway systems and development of other rapid means of transportation have made isolation as a policy for the community as obsolete as air transport and the Intercontinental Ballistic Missile have made it for the nation.

Suburban Consumer

The relocation of a large chunk of the American middle class from the cities to the suburbs has resulted in a comparable growth of stores and services to satisfy this lush new market. The list of goods and services which the new home owner will require is so extensive that it's fortunate for the builder that the owner doesn't know it before he takes title.

An automobile becomes a necessity for daily living, to get to the station, the supermarket, the dentist, and the Girl Scouts. In the city these can be reached by foot or public transportation, although most city dwellers hang on to their cars as a convenience, if not a necessity, despite parking difficulties. In the suburbs, however, the second car is the convenience, even if it is a jalopy which is parked at the station for most of the day. (Jalopies as well as good cars, eat gasoline, require repairs, and must be insured.)

Automatic laundry equipment must replace the city laundry or the centrally located apartment house laundry room. Gardening equipment and supplies can add up to quite a sum, particularly when power equipment is used on postage-stamp-size properties. There is suddenly room for a barbecue grill and a patio in the yard and a freezer in the kitchen. The house is bigger and needs more furniture. The wind blows freer, and storm windows and doors must be added. The basement and attic are wasted as long as they aren't finished, and of course the family soon finds a need for them.

The list of new services required in the suburbs also makes quite an addition to total business figures and quite a dent in the budget. For each house there is heating equipment to clean and service, additional electrical appliances to repair, plumbing to be maintained. Gardening services flourish all summer, and in many areas spraying services are required to clear the air of mosquitos, flies, gnats, and other presuburbanite inhabitants. The moving companies owe part of their prosperity to the fact that building in suburbia gave people a place to move to. Also the first house bought usually is not the end of the road. There is a high degree of mobility in suburbia; "Organization men" are transferred, and families outgrow their first homes either in size or by progressing up the income ladder to a point where they can afford a more expensive suburb. Not the least of the services born of the suburbs is paid for only indirectly by the suburbanite—the cost of studies to decide what he buys, why he buys it, if he goes to church because of his neighbor or his faith, why he becomes a Republican

when he moves to the suburbs, and which he hates more
—the lawn or commuting.

Suburban areas have higher family incomes and a
larger than average number of children, two sound reasons why they also have a higher expenditure rate for
goods and services. According to the consumer expenditure study done by *Life* magazine, the most lucrative
market is in the suburbs surrounding cities with more
than 50,000 inhabitants. Average household expenditures for goods and services run 30 per cent above the
national average. These areas, with 15 per cent of
the country's households, account for 19 per cent of
dollar expenditures. Some of the categories for which
suburbanites spend more are home furnishings and
equipment, home operation and improvement, recreation and recreation equipment (except spectator
sports), and automobiles, their use and maintenance.

A whole new pattern of distribution has arisen to
satisfy this demand. The shopping center which originated on the west coast before the beginning of the
Second World War has spread so fast since the end of
the war that today there are probably more than 1,000
in operation with more than 500 being added every year.
The recent growth has been so rapid that expansion will
have to slow down, at least temporarily.

They sell all the products a family needs, and frequently include branches of the nearby city's largest department stores, as well as national variety and apparel
chains. They have adapted themselves to the buying
habits of the suburban consumer, staying open three to
six evenings a week, doing nearly half of their business
in the evenings and on Saturdays when the family car
is available.

Between 1948 and 1954 retail sales in 45 metropolitan

areas increased 32 per cent in the suburbs and only 1 per cent in downtown areas. For the out-of-city residents suburban stores are easier to reach, present little parking problem, are less crowded, and pleasanter to shop in. They usually contain a sufficient variety of standardized merchandise like appliances and television sets and of the less highly styled merchandise like children's clothes, underwear, and sleepwear. But for really expensive items, fur coats, furniture, good jewelry, there is still a marked preference for the city store. Men's clothes usually make a poor showing in suburban stores because men do most of the buying and favor the city where they work. Suburban stores sell more than 60 per cent of children's clothes and cosmetics, but only 25 per cent of furs.

Business in the Suburbs

In addition to the growth of retailing, banking, and the multitude of service trades which are necessary to the suburban population, there has been a movement of manufacturing firms to the outlying areas. This movement has been called a "flight to the suburbs," but the label is inaccurate since it implies that the chief reason for plants to move has been to get away from the city— its congestion, high labor costs, and pressures. In individual instances these may have all been important factors, but more generally firms which moved or established themselves in the suburbs had outgrown the city in their space requirements. This does not mean that the city is losing its importance to the same extent for all kinds of business.

When a large manufacturing plant outgrows its space it cannot simply add on another piece in the same building as an office frequently does. As the manufacturing process is organized more and more into a continuous flow, companies will require large tracts of land for low buildings rather than the multistoried space available in a built-up city. If, in addition, it locates its suburban plant near a railroad siding or the interchange of a good highway, it will have easier access to large quantities of raw material than by way of the city streets.

Of course, this assumes that the firm is large enough to be able to supply economically some of the services for itself and its employees that are easily bought when needed in the city. This may include a cafeteria, parking lot, special buses from central points, emergency medical care, a private guard for the plant, a power generator, fire protection. It also assumes that the output of the firm is stable enough to warrant building, rather than enlarging and contracting rented space as needed. In addition, the product of the plant must be standard enough not to require frequent consultation with a varied group of specialists or close contact with a fluctuating market.

For the many small manufacturing establishments whose size and sales uncertainties make the building and maintenance of a suburban plant impossible, the city offers many advantages. Space can be rented or given up as needed. The large labor supply makes it easier to hire and fire as business warrants. Services for the business and employees can be bought in as small quantities as is necessary. If the firm's raw materials and product are unstandardized, it will be better off near a variety of sources of supply and customers.

The net result of these two different needs is that there has been a decline in the number of manufacturing jobs in the city, and a concentration of available jobs in smaller firms. In the Detroit area, for example, there were only 26 automobile plants with more than 100 workers located outside the city in 1939. By 1955 the number had increased to 218 plants. In 1929, 67 per cent of production workers in standard metropolitan areas were in central cities; by 1954 the proportion had declined to 59 per cent. In 1954 manufacturing firms in central cities had an average of 38 employees while the average number of employees in plants located in the suburbs around these cities was 62. The decline in manufacturing jobs has been partly offset by the increase in jobs in business service industries like finance and insurance.

For management, as well as for the small manufacturing firm, the city offers advantages which make it difficult for the suburb to compete, and it is common practice for large firms with plants in suburbs or small towns to have their main offices and show rooms in a large city. Here they have available lawyers, accountants, advertising agencies, commercial banks, economic and management consultants, commercial artists, printers, and the host of other business services which are carried out best on a face to face basis. Conversely, all these services need to be in the core of the city where they will be easily available to a heterogeneous group of customers.

In the early 1950's it seemed that management as well as manufacturing might be heading for the suburbs. Office space was scarce, inadequate, and excessively expensive. Since that time, however, a tremendous renewal program for the business districts of our large cities has got underway and it looks as if management will not follow manufacturing out of the city. The Union Carbide and Carbon Company is a good illustration of the pattern of split locality. In 1951 the company took options on a large tract of land in suburban Westchester. When building finally got underway in 1956 it was decided that the Westchester buildings would contain some sales departments, two laboratories, and a central utilities plant. The company still planned to build a Manhattan skyscraper for its home offices.

Future suburban growth and development may tend to break down some of the advantages of the city for small manufacturing and for business service firms. As the suburb becomes a city in itself, attracting more people and more types of industry, it can offer some variety of services and customers. But for some time to come the city will remain the best home for management, business services, and fashion industries.

Relation between City and Suburb

The distinction drawn between life in a city and its suburbs by means of a line on a map may be an unreal one except for government and tax purposes. It is possible, in some of our largest cities like Chicago and New York, to live in a section technically part of the city but more isolated from its core than one would be in a suburb of a smaller city. The trip to and from work may take as long and be as tiring, and the living may be as communal in its outlook.

The distinction should be drawn between the core of the city and the surrounding areas, the distinguishing features of the core city being the variety of its people, schools, restaurants, stores, and cultural facilities and the specialization of business and personal services. The suburbs can and often do provide excellent cultural experiences through local arts councils and adult education programs, and for millions this personal experience in a small community may be more rewarding than having the finest city facilities reasonably available but unused. But the suburbs cannot support or provide facilities for the top opera companies and symphony orchestras or house priceless art collections. They cannot build and support the equivalent of the Chicago Zoo or the New York Public Library. They don't have the customers for the "off-beat" restaurants, or the small stores dealing in hand-made, imported, and otherwise unstandardized merchandise, or students for all the specialized schools.

The fact that the function of the city is changing both in regard to business and as a residential area does not mean that it must lose all function. Historically, our cities have sprung up and grown rapidly with little planning or thought of function. They have started near sources of raw materials, near a port, along the river, adjacent to the railway line—frequently at some point where transportation facilities converged so that the growing city could act as a collection point for the products of the surrounding areas, establish industries to process them, and then act as a center for redistribution. It became a center where all kinds of work were available; it attracted migrants from other parts of the country and immigrants from other parts of the world, and it kept growing.

As the highway and motor vehicle began to supplement the railroad, penetrating country areas with a much wider spreading network of transportation facilities, it was to be expected that some of the functions of the city which depended on transportation facilities should spread out with the roads. As the car became a mass production commodity it was also to be expected that there would be less of a tie to the city as a home within reach of work.

The dispersion is well underway and will continue. Despite the temporary declines in marriage and birth rates during recession years, the long-term outlook is for continued growth in population. The large crop of babies born in the "baby boom" of the 1940's is just about reaching maturity, and the rate of family formations should spurt in the 1960's. There will be no satisfactory housing for these new families except by additional building in the suburbs, and this is where they are expected to go. The central cities are built up, and their population should remain relatively stable in numbers.

Business will continue to expand into the suburban areas as retailing and warehouses follow their market. Automation will also encourage dispersion since manufacturers will be less dependent on large labor supply centers and need more horizontal space. Offices, like insurance companies, which require a large force of clerical help will find the computers less attached to downtown shopping facilities than young girls are. Margaret Mead has suggested that the city will even lose its function as a center for administration as closed circuit television replaces conferences.

As the suburbs of one city spread they meet the suburbs of the next, and the pattern of development is rapidly taking the form of "strip cities" or "interurbias." (According to J. Walter Thompson Company an "interurbia" is defined as an area containing at least two adjacent cities of 100,000 population or more, or one city of 100,000 and three of 50,000 population. The connecting land may have no more than 25 per cent farm population and must have more than 100 people per square mile.) Such areas already run almost unbroken down the northeast coast from Maine to Virginia and along the California coast south from Los Angeles. In the Midwest, the urban area starts around Milwaukee, goes south to Chicago, and is moving east to meet the urban area moving west from Pittsburgh.

By 1975, 150 million people will be living in urban areas. The suburbs will have become increasingly independent of the core city for ordinary services, jobs, and recreation. Industrial workers, for example, will be able to reach several centers by way of the new network of roads that will encourage travel between suburbs as well as into the city. The original description of the suburbs, a place inhabited by people who work in a city but prefer not to live in it, will hardly be characteristic anymore.

However, if the core cities can solve their worst problems—traffic and slums—they can retain their preeminence as cultural and entertainment centers, and even as business centers, although in a more circumscribed area than has been true. Certainly the money and energy that are going into urban renewal for office buildings, hotels, and cultural centers all over the country—Philadelphia, St. Louis, Chicago, New York, Pittsburgh—is good evidence that the cities are far from giving up.

If the city is to remain a center of any kind, it must also be a place to live, not as it is now only for the very poor and very rich, but for a substantial section of the upper middle class. There are millions of people to whom the city is the only place to live, to whom the advantages outweigh the disadvantages. There are others who leave the city reluctantly because they cannot find comfortable living arrangements at reasonable rents.

These are the people who would be an asset to the city's finances; they pay comparatively high taxes and require less-than-average services. They would also support the concerts and art galleries and the variety of stores, keeping the city alive after five, and making it attractive to the suburbanites for special occasions and even week-ends and vacations.

But thus far, all the slum clearance projects have not stopped the encroachment of the slums. The continuing stream of low-income migrants overcrowd previously respectable neighborhoods much faster than new housing can be provided. Most of the private residential developments have shown little imagination in design and give little attention to the way in which people would like to live. Public or private, new housing seems designed for a race of cliff dwellers with no consideration of the fact that people prefer to live closer to the ground.

As we move toward a period of immense, decentralized cities, the importance of the core to the surrounding areas will depend largely on what special facilities it can offer, how convenient it is to get there, and how pleasant it is to move around inside. All kinds of new techniques for achieving maximum use of core areas have been proposed—moving sidewalks, enormous parking facilities to stop cars before they get to the central business district, underground delivery systems, elevated streets for pedestrians, residential areas which incorporate suburban amenities, greater use of helicopters—all possible if planning were large in scope instead of fractional.

According to Dr. Wilfred Owen of the Brookings Institution:

Every year houses, schools, streets, and utilities equal to the needs of four million people are being built in urban areas. If this rate is maintained, enough new city structures will be built in the next 25 years to rehouse all of the people, and all of the commercial, industrial, and cultural institutions now located in urban and suburban areas.

If building continues unplanned in both the city and suburb, it will prove to have been the most gigantic waste in our history.

7 SERVICE

At Your Service

Among all the revolutionary changes which have occurred in the last half century in American life, in the status of women, in technology, in the mushrooming of suburbia, in moral standards—all of which have been well publicized—one big change has gone practically unnoticed except for a few economic studies. It is a basic shift in our economic structure, away from dominance by the industrial or commodity-producing sector toward the growing importance of the service industries.

Perhaps the change has been relatively unnoticed because the story is hidden in statistics which do not have the popular appeal of the Kinsey reports and because it is not apparent to the casual observer, as is the tremendous growth in car ownership, for example. It has also been less dramatic, extending over many years, occurring slowly but persistently rather than explosively like suburban growth. However, the shift has now progressed to the point where its effects are obvious even to those who are unaware of the cause. It has become apparent during periods of economic recession, when prices, total employment, income, and sales hold up relatively well in spite of declining industrial activity.

Longer life, more leisure, and the pursuit of pleasure are all part of the growth of the service industries and are as good an index of a higher standard of living as the per capita measure of the number of telephones, bathtubs, and cars. The importance of the service sector, therefore, can be regarded as a new stage in the evolution of our standard of living. In the first stage, practically everyone—men, women, and children—was engaged in the production of goods. With technological advances the proportion of the population in the labor force declined, with women staying home away from the centers of production and more time allowed for children to get an education. As mechanization progressed further, income and the standard of living kept rising. There was time and money left after the absolute necessities of food, shelter, and clothing had been provided, and this resulted in a greater demand for services of all kinds. In the last decade alone, real, per capita purchasing power increased 19 per cent.

The proportion of the nonagricultural labor force engaged in the production of goods showed a long-term decline, while the proportion engaged in the service industries increased. Here's where we stand now.

• Employment in the service industries exceeds employment in manufacturing, contract construction, and mining combined. Today, approximately three-fifths of our nonagricultural labor force is employed in the industries generally classified as service producers—transportation, utilities, government, recreation, personal service, trade, finance, etc.

• In 1956, for the first time in our history, the number of white-collar workers exceeded the number of blue-collar workers. This does not imply that only white-collar workers are found in service industries or that all employees in manufacturing plants are blue-collar workers. There is overlapping in both.

In a study published in *Fortune,* it was shown that even in manufacturing industries, nearly one-fourth of the employees are nonproduction workers, that is, they actually perform a service. These include professional and technical personnel, management, clerical, and sales people. In ordnance production, for example, 41 per cent were nonproduction, in instruments and petroleum 33 per cent, in electrical machinery 30 per cent. Although no comparable data are available for what might be called production workers in the service industries (like the men who lay gas pipes or string telephone lines), it is apparent that there is an overlapping in the opposite direction as well.

• Service industries generate 57 per cent of our national income.

• Consumer expenditures for services (including housing) are 38 per cent of all consumer expenditures.

The growth of the service industries is part of economic growth and is not unique to the United States. Back in the late 1930's, an Australian economist, Colin

Clark, found that in the more industrialized countries of the world the proportion of employees in the service trades was high compared with underdeveloped countries like China and India. As machine production takes over, there is a rise in manufacturing employment; when this begins to level off, the service industries begin to provide an increasing number of jobs. We have reached this phase.

It may be an oversimplification to say that science and technology have been the cause of the growth of the service industries. Certainly many factors help to change our economic profile, but science and technology underlie all the important ones. Thus:

Urbanization of the population brought with it the need for many new services—communal waste disposal, fire and police protection, health services. But people flocked to the cities because the factories, railroad junctions, and jobs were there.

More leisure, resulting from a gradually declining workweek, brought with it a demand for recreational services—travel, hotels, motels, spectator amusements, movies, and theatres. But leisure came from the higher productivity of the mechanized factory.

Higher family income and more real purchasing power made it possible for tastes and desires to change, with an increased demand for the education and cultural activities formerly associated with the wealthy classes. Rising incomes were also made possible by higher productivity.

The aging of our population means a greater need for specialized geriatric services. Longevity has resulted from scientific progress.

However, the effects of technology on the bulk of the service industries do not hold for all. Technology in the home, in the form of automatic equipment, vacuum cleaners, polishers, and semiprepared foods, has decreased the need for domestic service and commercial laundries but greatly enhanced the position of the repairman. The installation of a computer in an insurance company may make a clerk obsolete but put a premium on the more highly trained programmer and the maintenance man.

Which Are the Service Industries?

It must be pointed out that it is not possible to make a rigid classification of industries into commodity-producing and service. The generally accepted meaning of the term "service industry" is an economic activity in which the product sold is primarily a service rather than a material commodity. The qualification "primarily" is important. There are few service industries whose product is completely service; those coming closest to it are the professions like law, accounting, and teaching. Beyond these, however, it is obvious that repair services include in their cost the price of very tangible repair parts, that telephone service includes the cost of equipment, and that hotel charges include the price of food. On the other hand, the manufacturing industries are also selling services. The cost of a package of frozen vegetables includes food preparation, package design, advertising, transportation, selling, all classified as services when they are the primary function of the company.

It is simplest, for analytical purposes, to follow the rather arbitrary government method of reporting indus-

try statistics, and to include in service industries transportation and public utilities, wholesale and retail trade,
finance, insurance and real estate, government, personal
and business services.

The list suggests the difficulty of discussing the service
industries as a group. We have here lumped together
the insurance company and the shoe repair man, the
doctor and the domestic servant, the banker, and the
retail clerk. There is too much heterogeneity in size of
organization, in income, in hours of work, to limit our
analysis to the group as a group.

At the end of the size scale we have the insurance
companies, telephone companies, public utilities, banks,
employing approximately 6.5 million people. At the other
end are the whole collection of small service establishments, the repair shops, beauty parlors, laundries, printing shops, photography studios, entertainment establishments, funeral services, which individually employ few
people, but collectively also employ about 6.5 million.
In between are the wholesale and retail establishments,
big and small, employing 11.5 million and the government (local, state, and federal) employing almost 7.5
million.

Business Services

Many of the everyday activities of business involve a
service performed by industry specialists. The automobile advertisement that you glanced at last evening, the
bulky envelope with a postpaid return card inviting you
to become a member of that special executive book club,
or the newspaper account of a company merger—all
involve business service specialists. An advertising
agency prepared and placed the automobile advertise-

ment; a direct mail organization prepared and even mailed the book club invitation; the company merger involved the services of lawyers, security analysts, researchers, public relations consultants, management engineers.

Some of these industries, such as industrial shop towel laundries, service business only. Others, the linen service laundries, for example, serve both business and consumers. Nevertheless, we have grouped a number of these industrial specialists but have taken into account those instances where a duality of service exists. Among the industries in this business service category are:

Wholesale trade—which dominates the business service group and employs more than 3 million workers.

Advertising and public relations.

Accounting and auditing.

Legal and other professional services—which includes such diverse groups as marketing organizations, management consultants, audio-visual experts, employee training directors, economic advisors.

Engineering and architectural.

Maintenance firms—who supply laundry service, dispose of waste, wash windows, maintain office machines.

Financial—including such services as banking, credit-collection, security and commodity brokers.

Insurance and real estate—including among others, title companies, community development organization, claims adjusters.

For the services performed by this group American business spends about 10 billion dollars annually, and

thus provides jobs for more than 3.5 million employees.
Until recently, college teachers held the distinction of
being the most minutely specialized of any of the professions; business service industries now contend for this
distinction. Among the many specialists available to industry are photojournalists, sales contest organizers,
press clipping bureaus, water consultants, indexers, tele-
phone-answering services, and combustion consultants.

Business services, like consumer services, are generally
not deferable, even in periods of lower economic activity. In fact, many businesses turn to these specialists
particularly during periods of recession in an attempt to
cut costs and increase sales. Business services thus have
a cushioning effect on the economy.

Government as a Service Industry

More than 15 per cent of the total nonagricultural
labor force is employed by the government—federal,
state, and local. The government's operations are ubi-
quitous. It is engaged in agricultural, mining, construction, even manufacturing, but more than 80 per cent of
all government employees perform services for individuals, industry, and agriculture. If we include the armed
forces (and this is a service too), some 95 per cent of the
federal, state, and local employees are working in a massive service industry.

An analysis of government employment in service
operations shows that:

More than one-third of all employees are teachers
or school administrators.
About one-third are engaged in public administra-

tion duties, operating the varied governmental service agencies, including such activities as the Bureau of Standards, Veteran's Administration, police, sanitation, and statistical analysis.

More than 7 per cent are in the postal department, a basic service in communications.

Over 6 per cent are engaged in transportation and utilities, both basic service industries.

Although many of the government employees perform services that only government supplies, such as law enforcement, national defense, and airways control, there is an increasing number who perform services which were at one time supplied almost exclusively by non-government groups, such as education, medical care, old-age and general welfare assistance. There has been a marked change in the individual's attitude toward what the government could or should do and a comparable shift in emphasis in government service during the last several decades.

Prior to the depression of the 1930's public services by the government, as we understand them today, were minimal. Government activity was concentrated in protective services (police and fire) provided by localities, and in roads and education provided by the states. The depression suddenly undermined the capacity of families to care for themselves, and the government had to step in and assume some of the functions previously performed by the family and private institutions. The need was too deep and widespread for a solution to be attempted by any other agency. One-third of the nation was "ill-housed, ill-clad and ill-nourished" and the other two-thirds weren't so prosperous either. Out of the

chaos emerged the philosophy that all citizens, regardless of means, were entitled to minimum standards of
health, working conditions, and housing.

The Second World War and its aftermath again altered
our attitude toward governmental services. The era of
full employment, rising incomes, and the growth of the
middle class resulted in a new definition of the word
"need." No longer did people think in terms of minimum standards but rather of optimum standards of service from the community. With money plentiful, the
community and the nation could afford to pay for more
and better service.

Despite the greater expenditures for these public services—health, education, recreation, welfare—demand
continues to exceed supply. At no time have we had an
oversupply of these services, and it appears that we
never will. Human needs are open-ended; new ones
arise when existing ones are satisfied.

Numerous factors have contributed to the growth of
government services since the beginning of the century.
The need for conservation, for example, resulted in the
creation of the National Conservation Commission as
early as 1909 under Theodore Roosevelt. The rapid expansion of industry and the growth of big business
brought on the Federal Trade Commission in 1914.
Many of the early agencies were regulatory, but some of
the later commissions combined both regulatory functions and industry service. The Civil Aeronautics Board
and the Civil Aeronautics Administration not only gov-
ern aircraft operation and control air traffic but also provide a service for the industry by compiling industry
statistics and engaging in research on air safety and
improved airport maintenance.

The disastrous consequences of recurring depressions,

particularly in the 1930's, took the government into services heretofore untouched—unemployment benefits, old age insurance, insuring deposits in savings accounts. At the same time the government expanded its services for small business, establishing advisory and financial assistance agencies to promote the growth of small business and to protect it in its competition with big business.

The creation of a "veteran class," as a result of two world wars and the Korean conflict, brought a further expansion of government services. Nearly $20 per capita is spent each year by the federal government to maintain these services, one of which has made the government the largest insurance company in the nation.

The tenuous peace and the cold war have added to the federal payroll the civilian employees of the military establishments, and the personnel of international agencies, assistance programs, and our generally expanded overseas services.

Also influencing increased government participation was the long-term decline in the number of children per family. More value was placed on each child and more was demanded of the health, education, and recreation services supplied by the government.

Greater emphasis is being placed on complete education for more children. In slightly more than a decade, from the end of the Second World War until 1958, the number of teachers employed by the government increased 90 per cent. Higher education has become increasingly important. In 1958 some 15 per cent of young Americans between the ages of 18 and 24 were enrolled in college as contrasted with less than 3 per cent back in 1900. Adult education is also an expanding government service, helping to meet the problems of the older worker and the new leisure mass.

Since the end of the Second World War federal employment has risen 25 per cent while state and local employment have risen over 50 per cent. The state and local increase has been a natural concomitant of our population increase and the continued shift to the cities and out to the suburbs. There is additional need for sanitation, water supplies, recreation facilities, police and fire protection, expansion of local transportation, more parks and beaches, inspection of local businesses. The phenomenal increase in the number of automobiles, the expanded highway network, the increased traffic and parking problems have created traffic divisions, research sections, larger highway patrols.

In the postwar period the ability of the citizens to pay for the expanded government services has contributed to their growth. Despite the perpetual cry about taxes, they wanted more and better government services and they could pay for them. The changed philosophy of the role of government and its relationship to the individual and family has turned the government into the greatest service industry in the nation. These services not only will be maintained but will also be increased by the current emphasis on education, slum clearance, juvenile delinquency, and research.

Growth and Productivity

In the years between 1919 and 1957 the nonagricultural labor force increased 96 per cent, because of rising employment in all of the service industries except transportation and public utilities. Mining employment declined 25 per cent, manufacturing increased 60 per cent, transportation and public utilities were up 14 per cent, wholesale and retail trade 145 per cent, finance, insurance, and real estate 109 per cent, personal and business services 210 per cent, and government employment 176 per cent.

The shift in emphasis in employment to services was made possible—and necessary—by the rise in productivity in agriculture, mining, and manufacturing, which permitted output to increase while the proportionate use of labor decreased. In the first half of the century, gross national product doubled, but the labor force remained almost a constant proportion of the population and worked a declining number of hours. At the same time, real purchasing power and the demand for services increased so that these industries were able to absorb the labor "left over" from manufacturing, mining, and agriculture. Productivity in services, lagged behind the others, increasing about 1.5 per cent a year compared with 2.5 per cent for all industries.

Productivity in service industries has recently been increasing, but it has still not caught up with industry as a whole. For any estimate of the future outlook we must separate the small repair shop from the insurance company for they have nothing in common when it comes to productivity possibilities.

The service industries which have been able to increase productivity are those which can take advantage of technological advances in the same way as a manufacturer does. The most recent developments in this area have been the business machines, and particularly the electronic data-processing machines, which have a future in finance, insurance, government, and large retail stores. There are also tremendous possibilities in warehousing where electronic controls and mechanical conveyors speed the flow of merchandise and machines keep track of the stock and type the bills.

The introduction of recent technological improvements, even in those service industries where it is possible, has just begun. Only a small number of banks, insurance companies, and other financial institutions have gone beyond the study stage, for office automation and automatic warehouses are still case histories. Less than 1 per cent of all expenditures for research and development are being made by the service industries, excluding the utilities. However, it is to be expected that automation will gain momentum and that productivity will increase much more rapidly in these industries in the next ten years than it did in the last ten. The rapid rise in employment, 35 per cent in ten years, will be slowed.

On the other hand, the multitude of personal and business service firms will hardly be touched by technology. Few of these firms are very large. For every firm with receipts of $500,000 or more, there are more than 100 with receipts under $15,000. More than half have no employees; another one-third have fewer than six employees. The few large firms are found among hotels, power laundries, cleaning and dyeing plants, and motion picture production. The establishments with no payroll at all were mainly among barber shops, beauty parlors, shoe repair, automobile, television, and radio repair and garment maintenance.

Because of the small size of these firms and the personal nature of so much of the work, we cannot expect much change in productivity. However, there will be an increase in demand for many of these services, particularly those catering to vacationers in cars and those who repair the multitude of electrical appliances and mechanical forms of entertainment which have become necessities. The same is true of the business services, accounting, law, advertising, management consultants, economic forecasters, poll takers; demand will increase, but productivity will lag. Employment in these industries will be an increasing proportion of total nonagricultural employment.

What Are We Paying For?

What services have we been spending more money on since the end of the Second World War? Can they be attacked as nonessential like the thicker pile on the rug or the engineered obsolescence of last year's car? Or do they represent the kind of improvement in our standard of living with which few would quarrel?

Many of our service needs stem directly from our purchases of commodities, like the tremendous wholesale and retail trade industries. Others are less directly but definitely related. We have been crossing over into the homeowner class at the rate of a million a year, largely because there is no adequate rental space available. We buy bigger and better space than we would be satisfied with if we were renting. We are fussier about the layout, the children need separate bedrooms, there must be play space indoors and out. In 1947 the rental value of owner-occupied nonfarm dwellings was 8.5 billion dollars; by 1957 we were spending 22 billion dollars for "renting" our own homes, an increase of 159 per cent.

Having bought the house, the new owner finds waiting for him the service company to clean and repair the oil burner, the plumber who puts the pieces together after the handy man takes them apart, the electrician to add outlets or increase the capacity, the gardener (after the owner has given up on the lawn), and the host of repairmen for the freezer, the disposal, the ironer, the dryer, none of which fitted into the rented quarters recently vacated. The need for utilities zooms. The house is too big for one telephone so one or two extensions are added and not infrequently two completely different lines for local and distant service. All the new appliances and the heating system take electricity or gas to run. Water is now required for the lawn as well as the household.

The statistics show the effects. In the ten years between 1947 and 1957 consumer expenditures for telephone, telegraph, cable, and wireless jumped 156 per cent, for gas and electricity 175 per cent, for water 109 per cent. Only a small part of the increase can be accounted for by an increase in costs. The price of utilities is under public control, and the increases during the ten-year period were around 25 per cent or less except for water.

The tremendous increase in the use of automobiles has created a host of direct and indirect service requirements. In 1957 we spent almost 15 billion dollars on new and used cars and an additional 4 billion on repair, greasing, washing, parking, storage, rental, and insurance. Travel tolls and motels, tourist courts, and trailer parks cost about 750 million dollars. Public transportation has suffered but all surveys indicate that Americans intend to stay with their own four wheels rather than returning to buses and trains.

Every purchase of a household appliance, small or big, brings with it an unwritten contract with the repair man. We are buying roughly 7 million television sets a year, 4 million washers, 2 million dryers, half a million dishwashers, more than half a million garbage disposers,

2 million air conditioners and 4 million vacuum cleaners —and the repair services are flourishing. Radio and television repair alone took 652 million dollars in 1957.

Our personal business services cost almost 16 billion dollars in 1957, an increase of 176 per cent in ten years. These services indicate a high level of consumer economic activity; they include brokerage charges, investment counseling, bank charges, legal services, and interest on personal debt. The largest single component was interest on personal debt, almost 5 billion dollars, and this category also showed the largest increase, 442 per cent in ten years.

We have increased our spending for a wide variety of personal services in the postwar period; in barber shops, beauty parlors, and baths 83 per cent; physicians and dentists 93 per cent; in hospitals 178 per cent; medical and hospitalization insurance 108 per cent; funeral expenses 55 per cent; religious and welfare activities 78 per cent; foreign travel 194 per cent; private education and research 116 per cent.

Checking through this very heterogeneous list, we find few items of the total 107 billion dollar expenditure which are open to a valid attack as superfluous. It can be argued, of course, that American women might be just as attractive if they spent less time and money in the beauty parlor, or that if we bought fewer gadgets we would support fewer repair men, or that if we bought less on installment we would pay less interest; but most of the big items in the service budget—better housing, education, improved medical care, religious and welfare activities—are part of a genuinely higher standard of living. To eliminate progress in these fields would be retrogression.

Economic Implications

There have been some striking consequences to the split in our economic personality between commodity production and services. It is no longer possible for the economist and the economic forecaster to make their analyses and forecasts on the basis of the health of the manufacturing segment alone. It is now possible for total employment to show an increase from one year to the next while manufacturing employment actually declines. This occurred between 1956 and 1957, when the decline in manufacturing employment was more than offset by increases in trade, finance, insurance, real estate, and miscellaneous services. It is also possible for the cost of living to continue upward in the face of increasing unemployment in the commodity-producing section.

The main reason for the difference in behavior between the two parts of our economy is that the purchase of many commodities, particularly durables, is deferable, whereas the purchase of most services is not. Under the threat of recession and unemployment, consumers will put off purchases of new cars, refrigerators, house furnishings, even clothes, and the price and production of these items will respond rather quickly to curtailment in demand. This delay, will add to the demand for services, since the appliance, made to do for another year, will be a more likely prospect for the repair man than a new one would have been.

It is more difficult to change the demand for housing which is bought or leased under contract; for education, an obligation ordinarily assumed for a stated period; for interest on a debt previously contracted; for repair of the appliances we have come to depend on; for the utilities without which we cannot run the household. Therefore, during periods of recession and depression, employment in service industries holds up much better than employment in manufacturing industries. At the depth of the depression of the 1930's, employment in the service industries reached almost two-thirds of total nonfarm employment. During the war the effect was just the opposite. The demand for war materiel shot up and carried employment in manufacturing with it. The relative importance of civilian services dropped sharply.

When the depression and the war had passed, the proportion of nonfarm employment in services resumed its steady upward climb. Between 1919 and 1957 the proportion increased from 51 to 61 per cent. Thus, today, our economy rests on a broader base and is less likely to topple quickly. The service industries, more stable because they are less subject to sudden changes in demand, supply substantially more than half our nonfarm employment.

This is the contribution made to the economy by the growth of the service industries. For basically the same reason that they contribute to stability of employment and income, they contribute to rising prices, even during periods of recession. While prices for services do respond with some lag to changes in the economic situation, the response during the postwar recession periods has been to advance more slowly rather than actually to decline. In the last ten years the price of services has risen considerably more than the price of commodities, 46 per cent compared with 18 per cent. The service prices which have jumped more than even the average of 46 per cent are automobile insurance, 76 per cent; transit fares, 114 per cent; obstetrical care, 57 per cent; hospital rates, 114 per cent; men's haircuts, 69 per cent. Short of staying at home and doctoring themselves, there is little consumers can do to cut demand—and so put a check on prices—of these services. In addition, since these are the very services which lend themselves least to automation, rising labor costs cannot be offset by increased production.

Do We Need More Goods? More Services?

The term "need" must be subjectively defined. There are people who "need" a fourth car or four guest bedrooms in a house, but no thoughtful appraisal of our economy can conclude that we really need more production of goods. No doubt we would be better off if we could build fewer war ships and more public transportation, and there may be serious questions about the equity of the distribution of our wealth of commodities, but there can be no question about the fact that we can produce enough to satisfy even our high standard of material demands. When a major advertising agency states that it will be necessary, through advertising and selling efforts, to make the consumer change his ideas of what satisfies him and raise his level of demand, it's time to take a good look at what we're selling and into what channels our tremendous capacity is going.

Are all of America's service needs so well supplied? Are our slums all cleared? Can every child get as much education as he can take without regard to his family's income? Do we pay our educators enough to attract competent people? Do we need a "Manhattan Project" in medical research? In a report for the Twentieth Century Fund, August Heckscher stated:

> Most of the public needs of the American community are supported marginally, often haphazardly . . . after private individuals have responded to all the lures and seduction to

which a dazzling merchandise subjects them. . . . Thus our society has been in the habit of deliberately shaping and stimulating the wants of private consumers: perhaps the same resourcefulness should be devoted by public leaders to stirring up the wants of people as citizens—to making them aware of deficiencies and opportunities in the public sphere.

It is good to be able to boast of our standard of living; we should also be able to boast of our standard of values.

0